Advice from the
Principal's Desk

Advice from the Principal's Desk

Five Pillars of School Leadership

David Franklin

JB JOSSEY-BASS™
A Wiley Brand

Published by John Wiley & Sons, Inc., Hoboken, New Jersey.
Published simultaneously in Canada.

Some material is adapted from previous work by the author. This content is incorporated into the following chapters:

- principalsdesk.org: Chapters 5, 13, 16, 18 27, 29, 30
- ascd.org: Chapters 7, 11, 24
- securly.com: Chapter 28

For general information on our other products and services or for technical support, please contact our Customer Care Department within the United States at (800) 762-2974, outside the United States at (317) 572-3993 or fax (317) 572-4002.

Wiley also publishes its books in a variety of electronic formats. Some content that appears in print may not be available in electronic formats. For more information about Wiley products, visit our web site at www.wiley.com.

Library of Congress Cataloging-in-Publication Data is available:

ISBN 9781394170883 (Paperback)
ISBN 9781394170890 (ePDF)
ISBN 9781394170906 (ePUB)

Cover Design: Wiley
Cover Image: © nuwatphoto/Shutterstock
SKY10062095_120823

To my wife, Cary,
and daughters, Mackenzie and Emerson,
your inspiration and love is woven throughout this book.

To my Mom,
the first teacher for thousands of children,
including my own.
Wish you were here.

Contents

Introduction   xi

PILLAR I: LEADERSHIP   1

Chapter 1:   Becoming   3

Chapter 2:   Principal Leadership Matters   7

Chapter 3:   Setting the Tone   13

Chapter 4:   A Top-down Approach Versus Collaborative
                 Approach   19

Chapter 5:   Be Seen   23

Chapter 6:   Professional Learning Communities (PLCs)   31

Chapter 7:   Looking at the Right Data   37

                 Tales from the Principal's Desk   41

PILLAR II: INSTRUCTION   47

Chapter 8: Instruction Matters   49

Chapter 9: It's Not How Much Time, But What You
Do with It   53

Chapter 10: Shifting from Teacher-Led to Teacher-Facilitated
Instruction   59

Chapter 11: Classroom Observations (Walkthroughs and
Instructional Rounds)   67

Chapter 12: Implementing Instructional Technology   73

Chapter 13: Assessment for Learning   81

Tales from the Principal's Desk   87

PILLAR III: COMMUNITY   93

Chapter 14: We're Not in Kansas Anymore   95

Chapter 15: School and Community Research   97

Chapter 16: Using Social Media in Schools   101

Chapter 17: Know Your Neighborhood   109

Chapter 18: Connecting with the Community   113

Chapter 19: One Call per Day   119

Chapter 20: Video Conferencing for All   123

Tales from the Principal's Desk   127

PILLAR IV: ATTENDANCE   131

Chapter 21: Get to School, Ferris!   133

Chapter 22: Get Butts in Seats   137

Chapter 23: Conducting Home Visits 141

Chapter 24: Creating Attendance Plans That Work 145

Chapter 25: Holding Parents Accountable 151

Tales from the Principal's Desk 157

PILLAR V: CULTURE 161

Chapter 26: Culture Is Everything 163

Chapter 27: Inclusion for All 171

Chapter 28: Creating a Safe Environment 183

Chapter 29: Sharing Your Own Story 191

Chapter 30: Creating a Collaborative Culture from
the Ground Up 195

Tales from the Principal's Desk 201

Conclusion 207
References 213
Acknowledgments 217
About the Author 219
Index 221

Introduction

The Journey

We often ask students what they want to be when they grow up. We use their ideas for slideshows, putting their dream profession on a whiteboard underneath their glowing smile. The professions that students pick range from doctor to football player, chef to engineer, teacher to lawyer, and everything in between. If you are lucky, you'll get to see a Batman or President of the United States among the answers. Do you know what profession is rarely brought up? School principal. I'm sure I could count on one hand the times that a child said they wanted to grow up to be a school principal. Furthermore, I am positive that being Batman had more interest than school leadership.

Many teachers start out in the education profession straight out of college, bright-eyed and bushy-tailed, ready to change the world. I was one of those teachers. I started out as a substitute teacher working at any school that needed me, in any subject, any grade level. My first assignment was in a second-grade classroom. It was a disaster. I remember coming home that afternoon exhausted, collapsing on the couch and falling asleep. However, the great thing about being a substitute teacher is that there will most likely be another job at another school tomorrow. My first regular teaching job was teaching music at a middle school in Poway, California, taking over for a teacher on maternity leave. After that year, I taught music in Carlsbad, California, for four years in my own classroom. I filled out my teaching schedule with periods of physical education and science/technology, and I loved it, but I knew I wouldn't stay for long.

I was lucky to find myself in a school that had only been open for one year before I was hired. The previous music teacher didn't work out and I was given the opportunity to create my own program. The only caveat was that I had to grow my numbers or I would not have a program to teach. I began the school year with around 30 music students – and I needed 100 students to continue the program.

Due to the nature of my main subject area, music, I had a knack for connecting with students who struggled with making connections at school. For many of these students, my class was the reason they came to school at all. Many of them had poor grades in several of their core classes, but were earning a legitimate A in my class.

Over the course of a few years, my program grew from a small, fledgling music program, to a robust powerhouse with over 150 students in five different bands. It quickly became the largest elective program at the school. I knew I was onto something when my incoming sixth-grade band kept growing year over year, ensuring that my older-grade bands would have large numbers as well in a year or two.

Due to the size and popularity of the program, we would routinely raise over $100,000 a year for new instruments, field trips, performances, equipment, and recording devices. We were able to secure partnerships with music stores, instrument makers, and even brought in Grammy Award–winning musicians to play for students and their families.

Earlier in my teaching career, I had begun to notice elements in the work that we do as educators that I couldn't quite understand. I felt that we were focusing on the wrong things and spinning our wheels trying to move forward but all we were doing was standing still. The same students kept excelling, while the same students kept struggling.

As time went on, I began to create an educational philosophy that would eventually become my foundation for the work I would engage in for a decade as a school leader. While I knew that the desire to move into administration was starting to grow inside me, I was not yet confident that the school leadership direction was for me. After all, I was a former musician with long hair, and taught an elective program.

Over the next few years, I took on different teacher leadership roles on campus such as sitting on our School Site Council, helping to determine funding allocations for teachers as well as serving as the Administrative Designee. This position was more compliance in nature as I would technically be the administrator in charge if both the principal and assistant principal were both out for the day. Luckily for me, and probably the school, I don't believe that situation ever happened.

My principal urged me to take the California principal licensure test, which I reluctantly did. I was quite content being a teacher, as I was at a great school with great colleagues and families. I hadn't thought about going into administration before. After growing my program and working with hundreds of students over the next few years, I didn't think it would hurt to get certified. Surprisingly, I passed on the first try, which kick-started my job hunt for assistant principal positions. I applied all over California, landing an AP job at a middle school in east San Jose. I was lucky enough to work with a seasoned principal who taught me the ropes, put me in challenging situations, and, unbeknown to me, trained me on the job to take over her spot. I was thrown into difficult conversations with teachers and parents, given some challenging teachers to evaluate, led a few fledgling committees, and grappled with attendance and student disciplinary issues. Most importantly, I learned from my mistakes. And let me tell you, I made a lot of them.

Moving into the role of principal happened sooner rather than later. At the end of my first year as an assistant principal, my principal was promoted to director of Student Services. As she was packing up her office, she casually told me to bring a suit to work the next day, just in case I needed it. It turns out that I did need it: I found myself changing into it midway through the morning after the superintendent's secretary called to tell me he'd like to see me at the district office.

Let's cut to the chase. He offered me the job, and the rest is history.

Or not.

The Good, the Bad, and the Ugly

I remember that I called a former principal of mine from my teaching days to tell him the news after returning to my school that afternoon. I will never forget what he told me. He asked if I was sitting in my new office. I told him I was. He said, "Look behind you. Is anyone there?" "No," I replied. He followed with, "Now you know what it is like to be a principal."

That's how my journey began. At 28 years old, I became a middle school principal.

My school had a variety of challenges. We worked with an under-represented community, challenged with poverty, gangs, and a distrust of the educational system. As I began my journey, I felt overwhelmed, unsure of myself, and wary of letting everyone down. Furthermore, there were staff members who were waiting for me to fail, as they were not too pleased with the district's decision to promote me given my young age and desire for change.

As teachers began to arrive back on campus to set up their classrooms for the upcoming school year, I was barraged with questions, complaints, and requests from everyone and everywhere. Teachers, staff members, and parents all descended upon me, like sharks smelling blood in the water.

I had never felt more alone in my professional life than those few weeks before school began my first year as a principal. There is no manual for this job. No amount of preparation, education, graduate courses, and professional development can prepare you for what it is like to step into the role of a school leader. I failed many, many times, but I got up each and every time, brushed myself off, and tried again. There were many sleepless nights, filled with tears, self-doubt, and fear. At the same time, there were also celebrations, feelings of accomplishment, pride, and collaboration. I took the wins when I could get them and viewed the losses as learning opportunities.

As I reflect upon my first couple of years as a principal, I remember the good times, bad times, and most vividly, the ugly times. Now that I am many years past those tumultuous times, I can see more clearly and recognize what I should have focused my time and energy on as well as how I wasted time focusing on trivial matters. It can be difficult for principals to focus their energy on the right areas in order to best impact student learning. Principals are thrust into having to navigate new relationships with teachers, staff members, different unions, district officials, hundreds of thousands of parents, and community members. It can be quite overwhelming.

I served as a principal for 10 years, spending five years at a middle school and five years at the elementary level. After leaving the principalship, I spent several years as a full-time professor of education, and worked as an education consultant in two education technology companies, working closely with districts to engage students at deeper levels, leading to better learning outcomes. I am also an associate of Dr. Robert Marzano, delivering leadership and school culture professional development to schools and districts across the United States.

The Principal's Desk Network

In 2016, I launched "The Principal's Desk." Originally, it was just a blog site for me to post ideas and articles that I wrote about school leadership, culture, communication, and instruction. After becoming frustrated with the lack of places educators could go to get advice, ideas, and support, I started "The Principal's Desk" Facebook group. It started out small with just a few hundred members with whom I had directly connections. After about four years, I had a few thousand educators in the group and I was thrilled that our numbers were growing. I remember posting announcements that "The Principal's Desk" group had surpassed 25,000, 50,000, and 75,000 members. Hitting 100,000 members was exciting and something that I could never have imagined just a few years prior. Within a year, "The Principal's Desk" blew past 200,000 members, serving educators from over 200 countries around the world. In this group, members share ideas, best practices, and stories from their schools. Many of the posts I see are from new principals, thrust into positions of leadership for which they were not fully prepared. Many of them are struggling, looking for a lifeline to help turn things around.

My goal in writing this book is to support these new principals in their journey and to have them learn from my mistakes as well as successes. It is important that principals are set up for success. Many sources indicate that around 20% of principals leave their positions every year. Schools need consistent leadership in order to maintain a constant vision of excellence. Sadly, many teachers report that in a span of just five years, they have worked with three or four principals. That is not a recipe for success.

The Five Pillars of School Leadership

This book will examine five pillars that principals need to focus on in order to support students, parents, staff members, and teachers through the academic process. These five pillars have been cultivated, revised, and perfected over the past two decades (Figure 0.1).

The five pillars are:

1. Leadership
2. Instruction
3. Community

4. Attendance
5. School Culture

This book will break down each pillar into three distinct areas: First, we will examine the research and data around the pillars, why they are important, and how they impact learning outcomes. Second, we will address different problems and solutions within each pillar. Lastly, we will dive into real-world examples of solutions at work in schools across the world.

Leadership: First and foremost, the ability to be a competent leader is a must for a school principal. The best leaders are those that get away from the top-down approach and work collaboratively with others to fulfill a common vision. Heavy-handed principals usually do not have a long tenure at their schools and rarely leave behind lasting change. School leaders must be visible, both in person and digitally. Principals need to get out of their office

Figure 0.1   Five Pillars of School Leadership

and be with teachers and students throughout the day by visiting classrooms, walking the cafeteria, greeting students in the morning, and saying good-bye in the afternoon. This is the only way to build rapport with different stakeholder groups. You can't build relationships hiding behind a closed door in an office. The same can be said for building a digital presence. It is not enough for principals to be visible in person anymore. Having a viable digital presence can help spread a positive narrative about both the principal and the school as a whole. School leaders should also be experts in creating a positive space for professional learning communities (PLCs). Through the use of PLCs, teacher groups can work together to build their own capacity as well as share best practices that will lead to increased learning outcomes. However, in order to have well-running PLCs, data protocols need to be in place and followed by all staff members. *Data* has become a four-letter word in education because it has been used to give both students and teachers a grade. The true purpose of data is to establish a starting point and to be able to see where a child goes on the learning continuum over time. We must be clinical, not critical, with our data.

Instruction: A strong instructional program is essential for a successful school. Principals need to focus on both the instruction occurring in classrooms as well as the curriculum being used by teachers and students. All students deserve to be taught using a proven and viable curriculum. That curriculum needs to be delivered with fidelity each and every day. Furthermore, that curriculum needs to meet the needs of all students, including children who are struggling and those who need acceleration. There is no one-size-fits-all curriculum model. Creating a student-centered approach will allow all students to have their needs met where they are, not where standardized testing states they should be.

Community: Many communities are centered around local schools. Education institutions serve students during the day and the community at large in the evening. It is vital that schools be transparent with the communities they serve as well as tap into local resources to deepen relationships. Parents need to feel welcome at their local school and have a say when it comes to school practices and district policies. If the community has a seat at the table, they will be more inclined to support the school through difficult times, including changes in funding and major disciplinary issues that may become public. Tapping into community resources for local experts, problem solvers, and sponsors is a great way to showcase a school in a positive light. This is also another opportunity to utilize social media and share the wonderful work of teachers and students at your school in collaboration with the community.

Attendance: A school can have the most wonderful teachers, the most caring staff members, and the most dedicated principal, and students will still be unsuccessful if they are not in school. Students can't learn from teachers when they are absent. According to the US Department of Education (2020) more than 20% of high school students are truant every year, and 14% of middle school students are also truant each year. In order for students to flourish in school, they must be present. Being in attendance can change a child's trajectory in life. Students who attend school regularly have a stronger connection to their teachers and peers. That feeling of belonging leads to higher levels of academic achievement. Focusing on increasing attendance is an integral element in school improvement.

School Culture: All of the preceding pillars culminate into creating a positive school culture for both staff and students. A school's culture can be thought of as a fine dining dish with leadership, instruction, community, and attendance being ingredients. It is important for school leaders not to confuse climate and culture. Climate refers to the current mood of the school. This can and does change day to day, week to week. The culture of a school refers to the overall and mutual feeling that one gets when walking onto the school's campus. It is seen in how people are greeted, how students treat each other, how staff treats each other, and how parents interact with everyone. A school culture is evident when walking onto a campus. It is also known throughout the community.

How to Use This Book

Each school leadership pillar will be broken down into three distinct areas: Research and Data; Problems and Solutions; and a Real-World Tie-in entitled Tales from the Principal's Desk (Figure 0.2).

The first section, Research and Data, will show the need and importance of the pillar as well as how it can influence a school's culture and overall student learning outcomes. The second section, Problems and Solutions, will address tangible issues or areas of focus that schools need to address within that pillar. Each section of this pillar will address four of these issues or focus areas and how to address them. Finally, Tales from The Principal's Desk will bring in examples from my experiences as a school principal from the good, the bad, and the ugly sides of my tenure. These will be real situations I found myself in and how I addressed them. I have changed the names in the book in order to preserve the anonymity of educators I have worked with.

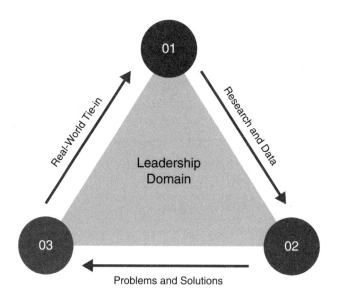

Figure 0.2 Leadership Domain

Here is the breakdown of each of the problems and solutions we will be addressing in all five pillars:

- Pillar One: Leadership
  - Top-down versus collaborative approach (teacher leadership)
  - Visibility (parking lot, yard, classrooms)
  - PLCs (what they are, what they are not)
  - Data analysis
- Pillar Two: Instruction
  - Teacher-led to teacher-facilitated (paradigm shift in ed)
  - Classroom observations (walk-throughs versus instructional rounds)
  - Technology integration (how to pick your tech)
  - Assessment (formative assessments lead to more data points)
- Pillar Three: Community
  - Communication (social media, interactive newsletters)
  - Knowing your neighborhood (shop local)
  - Maintaining parent support (coffee with the principal)
  - Tapping into community resources (universities, library, social workers)
- Pillar Four: Attendance
  - Getting butts in seats
  - Home visits (planning and execution)
  - Attendance plans (address the root problem)
  - Holding parents accountable (bringing in professional development [PD] and social workers)
- Pillar Five: Culture
  - Creating an inclusive environment (SpED, ELL, race)
  - Maintaining a safe campus (mental health, supervision)
  - Sharing successes (social media, local news)
  - Addressing problems together (collaboration)

The Many Hats of School Leadership

This book is for school leaders looking to make changes at their sites. Schools across the country and around the world need to be looked at more closely to see if they are achieving at high levels. As we tackle each of the five pillars, school leaders should reflect upon their own school and take stock of what is working and what needs to change. It is easy for school leaders to get bogged down in work that will not yield true change, leading to frustration and exhaustion. Please note that change is difficult and should not be undertaken on a whim or fleeting thought. True change is detailed, rigorous, and challenging. There will be blood, sweat, and tears. There will be days that you want to shut yourself in your office and write your resignation letter. There will also be days of elation, immense pride, and tremendous happiness.

Being a principal is a job of highs and lows, lefts and rights, ins and outs.

This book will share valuable insights into the secrets of success in school leadership and how to navigate this challenging landscape. Each chapter will give you opportunities to reflect, ask questions of yourself and your leadership team, and create an action plan for these high-needs issues. By addressing these five pillars, new principals will be able to successfully navigate the principalship and thrive within their school community.

I hope that this book will be a valuable resource as you start this exciting journey into school leadership. There will be treacherous roads ahead. School leaders encounter obstacles that they didn't even know existed. There is a reason why it is said that principals have to wear many hats that pull them in different directions. While I was a principal, I also served as a counselor, cook, furniture maker, painter, copy machine whisperer, firefighter twice (for real), private investigator, mail carrier, doctor, grant writer, wild animal catcher, and politician. With this type of a résumé, it is easy to lose sight of the true mission of our work. However, true school improvement and change is possible with the right tools, conversations, and focus.

I should know. I was a part of a school that did it. Twice.

Pillar I

Leadership

Chapter 1

Becoming

I became a principal at a young age – 28. After four years of teaching, my principal at the time encouraged me to go for my Administrative Services Credential and to start applying for administrative positions. After spending a few weeks considering my options, I went forward and got my Administrative Services Credential and started to apply for positions all over the state. To my surprise, I received an offer to become a middle school assistant principal. That summer, my wife and I packed up our lives and moved from Southern to Northern California.

From the beginning, I knew that this experience would be vastly different from teaching. I was immediately thrust into hiring decisions, fixing the master schedule, preparing classrooms for teachers and students, and meeting community members.

I was lucky enough to work with a veteran principal who was able to guide me during my first year out of the classroom. Calling that first year a bumpy ride would be generous. I felt lost, overwhelmed, and unprepared for the position. One of my first experiences in my new role was the hiring of new teachers, as we still had several vacancies to fill. I was new to this experience. At my former school where I was a teacher, we rarely had a vacancy come up. When we did, it was filled quickly with an amazing teacher. As we were conducting interviews at my new school, I was shocked by how unprepared most of the candidates were for both the interview process and the potential assignment itself. Sadly, we began the year with two vacancies and long-term substitute teachers.

None of my master's courses prepared me for what it would be like to be a school leader. That first year felt like five. I remember that it seemed like it rained every day. I'm not just talking about the physical act of rain, although we had an abnormally cold and gray winter and spring that year. I am talking more about it raining from the inside. I was lost in my new role. I was new to having parents in my face, disagreeing with every decision I made, as well as teachers banging on my office door, dropping problem after problem on my desk. I'm sure that I quit dozens of times in my head.

From day one, I found myself thrust into contentious parent meetings, disciplinary hearings, suspension and expulsion meetings, and teacher evaluations. Gone were the days where I worked with smiling and eager students. I now began and ended each day patching up huge problems with Band-Aids, dealing with disciplinary issues, and completing endless compliance tasks. The job of a school leader is lonely. Classrooms are filled with noise and the hustle and bustle of learning. An administrator's office is quiet and muted. I felt defeated.

If you are feeling the same way, you are not alone.

As the days turned into weeks and weeks into months, I found myself less overwhelmed and lost. I listened and watched my principal work, solve problems, and create solutions for both teachers and students. As a young assistant principal, I did my best to make a positive impact on the school, knowing that one day I would be standing in the shoes of my principal, leading a school, for better or for worse.

Little did I know that I would get my opportunity sooner rather than later. My principal was on the short list for a director position in the district. After a quick round of interviews, she was given the job and announced that she would accept the offer. The principal job opening at my school was immediately published. I did not apply, nor was asked to apply. Several candidates were interviewed, including a principal from a neighboring district that my principal had worked with in the past. She was offered the position and took a tour of the school, meeting me along the way. She seemed very competent, friendly, and connected to the community.

She turned down the job the next day.

As the story goes, she did not want to switch districts and was being considered for a principalship at another school. That meant that my school was still without a principal. One afternoon, my principal asked me if I was interested in the position. I said I was, but wasn't sure if I was ready for it. In hindsight, I knew I wasn't ready for it. However, I did not want to pass up the opportunity to make the leap into the principalship. It could be years before the offer would come my way again.

I could tell that conversations were happening behind the scenes. One afternoon, my principal told me to bring a suit to work the next day as I might need it for something. That next day, I was summoned to the superintendent's office. I had only met my superintendent a few times and never spoke with him one-on-one. I quickly changed into my suit in the small bathroom in the office and drove the three miles to the district office. I walked into the building and over to the superintendent's office and told his secretary that he was expecting me. She said that he was waiting for me and that I could go right in.

My superintendent greeted me when I walked in the door and he asked me to have a seat at the conference table.

Then, he asked me if I wanted the job.

I said yes.

At the ripe old age of 28, I became the next principal of my school. I was terrified, excited, and trepidatious all at once – as well as sure that I had made the biggest mistake of my career. There was no way that I was ready for this.

I spent the summer reading leadership books and preparing for the school year. No one knew that I was the new principal. As teachers began to trickle back in at the end of the summer, they all asked who the new principal was. None of them ever considered that it would or could be me. That hurt, but I understood. I was young, inexperienced, and unsure of myself. When it was publicly announced that I would be the next principal of the school, the news was met with skepticism by both parents and teachers. I knew early on that I would have to establish myself as different from my predecessor, even though she was well liked and respected by everyone.

I couldn't rely on years of experience in administration or my experience in the classroom.

I needed to bring something different to the table.

What Now?

Making the move to administration can be an overwhelming experience. It is not a decision that should be taken lightly. Talk it through with your spouse, partner, family, and friends. There will be school districts that are only looking for a seasoned veteran administrator or teacher with 20+ years of experience. However, there will be others that are looking for new blood, new ideas, and new perspectives.

Here's how to get started:

1. Connect with district administrators online through LinkedIn and other social media. Respond to their posts as often as possible. This way, they will start to get to know you even before your name comes across on an application.
2. Go down to the district office and say hello to the HR director in person. Most administrative positions get dozens if not hundreds of applications. You want to make yourself stand out in any way possible.
3. If you are already working in the district you want to become an administrator in, sign up for committees, boards, and task groups. This will give you exposure to district administrators and site leaders.

Chapter 2
Principal Leadership Matters

L eadership takes on a lot of different forms. Here are some of my favorite quotes from some well-known leaders from different industries:

Leadership is the capacity to translate vision into reality.
—Warren Bennis

The function of leadership is to produce more leaders, not more followers.
—Ralph Nader

Leadership is not about being in charge. It's about taking care of those in your charge.
Simon Sinek

The role of leadership is to transform the complex situation into small pieces and prioritize them.
—Carlos Ghosn

Good leaders inspire people to have confidence in the leader, great leaders inspire people to have confidence in themselves.
—*Eleanor Roosevelt*

The ultimate measure of a leader is not where they stand in moments of comfort and convenience, but where they stand in times of challenge and controversy.
—*Martin Luther King Jr.*

The best leaders are those most interested in surrounding themselves with assistants and associates smarter than they are.
—*John C. Maxwell*

The challenge of leadership is to be strong, but not rude; be kind, but not weak; be bold, but not a bully; be thoughtful, but not lazy; be humble, but not timid; be proud, but not arrogant; have humor, but without folly.
—*Jim Rohn*

Leadership and learning are indispensable to each other.
—*John F. Kennedy*

The Wallace Foundation conducted a variety of studies about the importance of the principalship. Here's what they found.

Principals really matter. Indeed, given not just the magnitude but the scope of principal effects, which are felt across a potentially large student body and faculty in a school, it is difficult to envision an investment with a higher ceiling on its potential return than a successful effort to improve principal leadership. (Gissom, Egalite, & Lindsay, 2021)

We also know that around 20% of all principals leave their role each year. That number is slightly higher in high poverty areas. Principal turnover leads to teacher turnover. When a school's staff comes and goes through a revolving door, it is impossible to build a strong culture focused on student achievement and well-being.

School leaders leave their roles for a variety of different reasons. Principals routinely face high levels of job stress, which can lead to burnout and exhaustion. They also may not receive adequate support from their superiors or colleagues, which can make their job more difficult and isolating. With increased emphasis on test scores and other measures of student achievement, school principals may feel they are under more pressure to produce positive results, which can be overly challenging and stressful. Assessments are not the only stressors principals face. School principals are responsible for managing multiple areas of a school, including budget, curriculum, staffing, and student discipline, which can be overwhelming. Having limited autonomy to make decisions about school policies and procedures can be frustrating and demotivating, leading to the desire to look outside their current position.

It is also important to note that the average tenure of a principal at a school site is four years. Four years is barely enough time to collaboratively create systems that work for both staff and students. The first two years are spent understanding the current culture of both the community and the school as well as identifying systems and procedures that need to be updated and strengthened. This means that a school is just finally coming together before the principal leaves, forcing the school community to start back at square one and begin the process all over again with the new principal.

This type of instability leads to teacher turnover. Currently, the teacher turnover rate is hovering around 8% per year. While that might not seem like a lot, we also need to consider the number of teachers who move schools or take another type of position within the district. When this movement is factored in, the attrition rate goes up to 16%.

I experienced this unfortunate data firsthand, as I would be this school's third principal in five years. My teachers were very wary of me when I announced that I would be taking over the principalship. While most of them didn't say it to my face, the phrase "this too shall pass" was used a lot when I started. Additionally, several teachers remarked that they had worked with over 10 principals at the school and that I probably wouldn't stay long. That was definitely not the way I was hoping to get started.

The role of the principal is undeniably linked to student achievement. While principals are not responsible for the direct instruction that students receive, they influence the learning environment in a variety of important ways.

Principals need to communicate a clear and compelling vision for instruction that is aligned with the school's mission and goals. This can help to establish a shared understanding of what high-quality instruction looks like, and to set expectations for teachers. Coaching, mentoring, and opportunities for collaboration and reflection need to be tied to the current instructional realities and needs occurring in classrooms.

You will need to be able to model effective instructional practices themselves, demonstrating the types of teaching strategies and techniques that principals want teachers to use in their classrooms. In addition, take the time to encourage teachers to take risks and try new approaches to instruction, while providing a supportive environment that allows them to experiment and learn from their experiences.

What Now?

New administrators should never embark upon this journey alone. While there will be directors and assistant superintendents who will help to guide you, there are a few other avenues to explore.

1. Find a mentor outside of your district. Sometimes, having a fresh perspective from someone who is on the outside looking in can be of great help to new administrators. They will help you not miss the forest for the trees.
2. Network, network, network. In today's social media landscape, educators can easily connect with other educators around the world to share best practices, vent frustrations, and celebrate

successes. "The Principal's Desk" Facebook group is one of the largest groups of educators in the world.

3. Connect with another principal who is well respected and emulate their mojo. Just as when you were starting out as a teacher, emulating another administrator will help you stay on the right path before you are able to deviate and create new directions on your own.

Chapter 3
Setting the Tone

The role of the principal is undeniably linked to student achievement. While principals are not responsible for the direct instruction that students receive, they influence the learning environment in a variety of important ways.

We set the tone.

Culture influences everything that goes on in schools: how staff dress, what they talk about, their willingness to change, the practice of instruction, and the emphasis given student and faculty learning (Deal & Peterson, 1994; Firestone & Wilson, 1985; Newmann & Associates, 1996).

Principals influence everything from actual instructional practices to technology use, to lunchtime (both student and staff), to communication, and areas of focus. I have said for a long time that a visitor can feel the culture of a school from the minute they step foot onto a school campus. From the first glances of the school grounds to the first sounds of both student and staff voices, a school culture can be summed up quickly and, for the most part, effectively.

Picture walking down the halls of a school with students and staff passing by you on either side. What do they look like? Are they smiling? Is anyone saying good morning to someone else? What do the halls look like? Are there positive messages flanking the walls? Are there examples of student work displayed for all to see?

Teachers directly control how their classrooms are run. Principals directly oversee everything else. That positive tone is set by the principal.

Or not.

Have you ever walked onto a school campus where everyone looks miserable and no one acknowledges anyone else? In addition, is the overall look of the school unremarkable and monotone? If it is, I can just about guarantee that the school is struggling academically, as student and staff morale are barely on life support.

Setting the tone is achieved by modeling what you expect of others. It doesn't cost any categorical funds to say good morning and smile when walking past students and staff in the morning. This is the easiest and cheapest way to set a positive tone. However, if you aren't willing to do this, then please close this book and begin looking for another line of work. Don't be mistaken, principals are chief culture officers (CCOs).

Another job of the principal or CCO is developing teachers and staff members. Many teachers are hired straight out of credentialing school. They are bright-eyed and bushy-tailed, and totally unprepared for teaching in the real world. Much like a principal's first year, a teacher's first year or two can be filled with tears, apprehension, self-doubt, and frustration. Principals must be there to coach these teachers as well as be their biggest cheerleaders. In thinking back to every teacher whom I hired over the years, there wasn't one of them that I didn't want to be successful. In addition, I never let a teacher go whose failure I felt responsible for.

Teacher development is essential. No one walks in the door an expert. No one leaves an expert, either, because kids are always changing. The question is, how do you develop teachers when there is so much on everyone's collective plate?

A Three-Pronged Approach

I recommend a three-pronged approach:
- Instructional rounds

- Mindful mentoring
- Tangible models

Instructional Rounds

Instructional rounds help teachers by observing what is working in other classrooms as well as what doesn't work. I always encourage teachers to "steal" ideas that they see during rounds to use in their own classroom. After all, isn't imitation the sincerest form of flattery? It also gives teachers the opportunity to see what happens in classrooms around campus. Regardless of the subject or grade level, good instructional practices can be adapted for any situation.

Mindful Mentoring

All new teachers deserve a great mentor. They need someone to bounce ideas off and to ask for assistance without judgment or evaluation. While new principals often want to be the knight in shining armor for new teachers, it is better that teachers connect with a peer. Even in the most carefully crafted environments, there is still an element of evaluator and evaluatee when the principal is involved that can never be fully expunged. Mentoring can be set up with formal meetings bimonthly as well as informal meetups and classroom observations conducted by the mentor. A mentorship also creates strong bonds between staff members, enhancing job retention and overall satisfaction.

For many new teachers, the first year of teaching can be overwhelming and stressful. Strong mentors can provide emotional support by listening, empathizing, and offering encouragement. Mentors can share practical knowledge and tips based on their own experience, such as classroom management strategies, lesson planning techniques, and assessment methods. This is especially advantageous, as you can't be in more than one classroom at a time! Mentors can demonstrate effective teaching practices by modeling lessons and instructional techniques. This can encourage new teachers to develop a clear understanding of what effective teaching looks like in practice. New teachers can get feedback on their instructional practices, helping them to identify areas of strength and areas for improvement.

Most importantly, mentors can support new teachers to navigate the school culture, including policies, procedures, and expectations. They can also introduce new teachers to other teachers and staff members, encouraging them to feel more connected to the school community. Choose your mentors wisely. You do not want new teachers to be influenced in a negative manner by staff members who are critical of the direction of the school.

Mentors can also guide new teachers to build self-confidence and self-efficacy by providing positive feedback and celebrating their successes. This can serve new teachers in feeling more assured of their abilities and more motivated to continue improving. This, in turn, can lead to higher teacher retention rates and job satisfaction.

Tangible Models

I have never been a fan of giving teachers just a theoretical teaching education. Understanding different philosophies of education isn't a bad thing, but I would want teachers armed with some more tangible ideas when they are standing in front of a classroom of 30 students. Unfortunately, many teacher preparatory programs rely heavily on theoretical teaching, rather than practical application. Instead of launching into the "why we do this," let's start with a simple "this is what we do." The "why" will come in time. Concrete examples make concepts more accessible. When teachers are presented with concrete examples, they can better understand how abstract concepts apply in real-world situations. This makes the ideas more accessible and easier to apply in their own teaching. Tangible examples demonstrate practical application of the concept and show teachers how theoretical knowledge can be put into practice, which helps them to understand the practical implications of the concepts they are learning.

Concrete examples can be adapted to fit the specific context of a teacher's classroom, making them more relevant and useful for teachers' own teaching practice. In turn, this can encourage teachers to retain new knowledge and concepts by providing a context for their learning. When teachers have a clear understanding of how a concept can be applied, they are more likely to remember it and be able to apply it in their own teaching.

At every school there are veteran teachers with decades of experience who are amazing educators in every area: instruction, classroom culture, classroom management, creating relationships. . . and then, there are veteran teachers who struggle with all of those same elements as they have never been provided the right mentoring or support, but just passed on from year to year. Supporting veteran teachers who may be struggling is crucial for their well-being and professional growth. However, this task can be quite daunting for a new principal with far fewer years in education than the teacher. Support of this nature must be thoughtful and empathetic.

Principals should create a safe and nonjudgmental space for veteran teachers to express their concerns, frustrations, or challenges. Chances are, they have seen the school environment change over the years and might be dealing with some resentment or frustrations because of it. Regular check-ins or one-on-one meetings can provide opportunities for teachers to share their struggles. Principals should actively listen, validate their experiences, and offer understanding and empathy.

Providing targeted professional development opportunities for veteran teachers to enhance their skills and address specific areas of need is vital. Often, professional development opportunities are created based on the needs of new teachers. Pairing struggling teachers with experienced mentors can offer them valuable guidance and support. Encouraging this type of collaboration among teachers can be beneficial for struggling veterans. Principals can facilitate collaborative learning communities or teacher-led professional learning groups where experienced teachers can share their expertise and provide support to their struggling colleagues. This promotes a sense of camaraderie, shared learning, and a supportive network within the school.

Some veteran teachers struggle with their well-being and work–life balance. Encourage them to practice self-care, set boundaries, and maintain a healthy work–life balance by exploring options such as flexible scheduling, reducing nonessential administrative tasks, or providing additional resources to alleviate the workload.

Struggling veteran teachers often get lost in the shuffle and are rarely acknowledged for their achievements and growth. We need to recognize their efforts and improvements, both privately and publicly. Positive reinforcement and appreciation can boost their morale, motivation, and confidence, leading to a better work experience and better student outcomes.

What Now?

Think about the kind of school you would want your children, future children, or family member to attend. The neighborhood or zip code your school is located in does not determine the culture. School leaders and teachers, working with parents, set the tone. It can be challenging to know where to begin when setting the right tone. Here are a few ideas to get you started:

1. Always practice what you preach. Make a point to say hello to everyone you walk past, especially teachers. This is a fundamental element in setting the right tone. Start here.
2. Break down barriers by having teachers visit other teachers during the school day. Teachers often work in isolation, siloed by departments, grade levels, and proximity to each other. Budget in advance for roving substitute teachers and schedule these visits well in advance.
3. Connect new teachers with positive mentors. If you don't, negativity will find them. The hiring of new teachers gives you the opportunity to conduct a reset. Don't waste that opportunity by losing them in the first few months of the school year when they need the most support.

Chapter 4

A Top-down Approach Versus Collaborative Approach

Some schools are set up as democracies while others are more like dictatorships. Another way of looking at it is to compare the leadership styles of Darth Vader and Obi-Wan Kenobi.

Darth Vader: powerful, frightening, larger than life, the face of the Dark Side, planet destroyer, ruthless, impatient.

Darth Vader can be characterized as an authoritarian and autocratic leader. He exercises strict control over his subordinates, demanding unwavering loyalty and obedience. He uses fear, force, and intimidation to maintain discipline and order, and is not afraid to use violence to achieve his goals. His leadership style is characterized by a "command and control" approach, in which he gives orders and expects them to be carried out without question.

Vader's leadership style is also characterized by a focus on results and efficiency. He is willing to make difficult decisions and sacrifices to achieve his objectives, and is not overly concerned with the welfare or feelings of his subordinates. He is willing to take risks and act decisively to achieve his goals, even if it means going against established protocols or risking the lives of others.

Does that sound like any school leaders you know?

Obi-Wan Kenobi: builds up others, shares knowledge, is ethical, does the heavy lifting when needed, is in control of emotions.

Obi-Wan Kenobi can be characterized as a transformational leader. He is a mentor and role model to his subordinates and encourages them to reach their full potential. He sets high expectations for his followers and provides them with the support and guidance they need to achieve their goals. He is known for his wisdom, patience, and ability to inspire others.

His leadership style is characterized by a focus on collaboration and teamwork. He values the opinions and contributions of his subordinates and encourages them to work together to achieve common goals. He creates a positive and inclusive work environment, where everyone feels valued and respected.

Another notable aspect of Kenobi's leadership style is his focus on ethics and values. He holds himself and his subordinates to a high standard of moral and ethical behavior and is not afraid to speak out when he sees injustice or wrongdoing. He is committed to doing what is right, even if it means going against established norms or protocols.

Same question: Does that sound like a school leader you know?

Now, whom would you rather work with? Whom would you rather go to with a problem or when something didn't go right? Remember what happened to Admiral Ozzel? Remember? He failed Vader for the last time and was dispatched when he came out of hyperspace too quickly. He could've used some strong mentoring. Sadly, he didn't get it, and most of us don't remember his character at all.

Principals who lead with a top-down approach will have a shorter tenure than principals who are collaborative. Decisions made behind closed doors create an environment of distrust with staff members and parents alike. Establishing buy-in under these circumstances is extremely challenging and is often achieved through fear and intimidation. This creates a poor school culture.

You will not see a lot of smiling faces and welcoming salutations when walking down the halls of these schools.

A top-down approach in school leadership creates a hierarchical management style where decisions and directions come from the top level of leadership, then passed down to lower levels of leadership, teachers, and students. This approach has been criticized for several reasons that can contribute to its ineffectiveness in creating a positive learning environment. In a top-down approach, decision-making is centralized at the top level of leadership, with little input from teachers or students. This lack of participation can lead to a lack of ownership and investment in decisions, leading to lower morale and engagement among teachers and students.

It also relies on a one-size-fits-all approach, which can be inflexible in addressing the unique needs of individual teachers and students. This rigidity can limit creativity and innovation in teaching methods, curriculum development, and other educational initiatives. Communication tends to flow in one direction, with leaders communicating their directives to teachers and students, but little opportunity for feedback or open dialogue. This can lead to misunderstandings and resentment among teachers and students and can hinder problem-solving efforts.

There can be a resistance to change as lower levels of leadership and teachers may feel alienated from the decision-making process, leading to a lack of support for changes being made. This can slow down the pace of progress and limit innovation.

Overall, a top-down approach in school leadership may not work because it can limit input, flexibility, communication, and progress, resulting in a less effective learning environment. It is important for leaders to consider a variety of approaches, including collaborative and participatory models, to create a positive and engaging educational experience for all students and teachers.

Principals who lead with a more top-down, authoritarian approach often have a few select followers who do everything they can to push the agenda forward. This leads to nepotism, resentment, and the wrong people invited to the decision-making table hidden behind closed doors.

Daniel Bauer (2022), author and CEO of Better Leaders, Better Schools, writes, "Your presence (your energy) impacts every aspect of the school—most importantly, the culture. If you are experiencing a toxic environment, that is on your shoulders."

Seth Godin (2021) says it this way . . .

"You get the culture you deserve."

What Now?

It is important not only that teachers feel like they are a part of the decision-making process, but that they are truly a vital element in that process. This can be tricky when first stepping into a school that needs a cultural revolution. Here are some ideas that work:

1. Find your team. It is important that you have a few teachers in your corner. These teachers will be your go-getters, your students' favorite teachers, and the ones who remain positive despite the amount of adversity they face.
2. Find your intermediaries. These individuals are teachers who live on both the positive and negative sides of the fence. While they are open to trying out new ideas, they also can get stuck in their old ways and enjoy a gripe session with the best of them. However, these are teachers who can spread change to your more "difficult" teachers, as they will listen to them more than they might listen to you.
3. Find your counterpoint. While it might seem counterintuitive, always ensure that you are working directly with one person with whom you do not see eye-to-eye. The goal is not to flip this person into one of your go-getters, but to act as an intermediary. Negativity can bring down an organization's culture. It is vital you move them forward, but it is not necessary to turn them into a champion. To be honest, that probably won't happen anyway. However, through diligent communication and trust-building, you can bring them to a point where they do not say no to everything.

Chapter 5
Be Seen

With everything principals have to do throughout the day, one of the most essential elements of the role is visibility. Students interact with teachers all day long. However, do they ever interact with their principal? If they do, how often? It is vital that principals be very calculated when it comes to the notion of visibility. It is important for students, staff, and parents to see and interact with the principal on a regular basis. It should not be a one-off event or sporadic experience.

A principal's visibility assures students that there is someone in charge, someone to whom they can go if they are experiencing difficulty, someone they can trust. Being less than highly visible erodes a school's climate and may have students wondering if the school really has a principal. Practicing being approachable and visible can easily be woven into the principal's daily schedule (Ruder, 2007).

You've Got to Rule the Parking Lot

The mere mention of a school's parking lot can weaken the knees of even the most seasoned educator or parent. For new principals it can be downright terrifying. There is never enough parking, parents routinely disobey traffic laws and common sense on a daily basis, and children who are respectful and responsible all day long seem to always become mesmerized by the thought of playing Frogger with cars. Let's not talk about how some parents never pull their car forward enough. Being present at the beginning and end of the day in the parking lot is a great way to let all the parents know that you are out there making everyone safe and wishing your students a good rest of the day. These short interactions can mean everything. They will also give you the opportunity to connect with parents, especially the ones who are difficult to track down for a meeting.

Social media often gets a bad rap due to its misuse as well as adolescents' dependence on it. However, social media is a great way to reach beyond just your school community. Try setting up a school Twitter and start sharing out all the wonderful things that happen each and every day. Don't like Twitter? . . . try Instagram, Facebook, Remind, or Snapchat . . . There are endless possibilities. These updates take just seconds and can provide parents with a strong connection to the school and you. As a parent myself, I love seeing pictures from inside the school so I can get a better sense of what my children are doing. And, every once in a while, I see my own children in a post. While I can't be at my children's school to volunteer, I appreciate being able to get to look behind the curtain and see some of the great things they are involved with.

Students love it when the adults in their lives interact with them on their level. Every day, parents ask their children what happened to them at school that day. Principals need to be mentioned in that conversation. Unfortunately, they rarely are. Think about it. If you have kids, when was the last time they came home gushing about how cool their principal was at school that day? Yeah. Never.

Here are some ideas to get the ball rolling:

1. Join a lunchtime basketball game.
2. Share Minecraft missions.
3. Debate current movies and music.
4. Talk about the game last night. Any sport will do.
5. Ask students to show you what they are learning about.

Remember, active principals are popular principals. You don't have to be Michael Jordan for students to be excited about you joining their basketball game.

When principals play sports with their students during recess, it provides an opportunity for them to build positive relationships with their students. This can help to improve trust and communication between students and their principal, which can lead to a more positive school environment overall. It also models healthy behaviors and shows that physical activity is an important part of a healthy lifestyle. This can inspire students to be more active and take care of their physical well-being. Students can also learn how to work together toward a common goal, and this can help to improve their social skills and ability to work in groups.

Playing sports with their principal can be a fun and exciting experience for students, and it can help to boost morale and school spirit. Students can feel like they are part of a larger group and that their principal cares about them and their well-being. This can help to create a more inclusive and supportive school culture.

If sports isn't your thing, connect with students over music.

One interesting fact about me is that I love hard rock and heavy metal music. I have also been a lifelong musician and played in bands throughout college and beyond. I have the distinct honor of being dropped from an opening slot with Lenny Kravitz because he didn't "like" our sound. I also have gotten the opportunity to play on stage with members of Metallica, Testament, Slayer, and Faith No More, but that's another book.

When I was a principal, I often connected with the kids wearing metal sweatshirts and T-shirts. The scarier the better. These kids were often loners and a bit socially awkward. I was the one person on campus who could go up to them and say, "Hey! Are you going to see Meshuggah when they come to town next month?" I would often get wide-eyed stares that translated to, "How do you know this band? You're a boring principal! It's not possible!" Oh it was. I could riff the same way with movies. Connecting with students at their level with their interests is a sure-fire way to have students go home and tell their parents about you that night.

Grab a hairnet and get to work in the cafeteria. One of my favorite pastimes is to help students select a hot lunch. If you can make a school lunch sound appealing, then you can accomplish anything. I had songs I would sing about the cheeseburgers, quesadillas, and pizza pockets. I also was making sure that everyone was eating lunch as well as keeping track of which students were low on their meal accounts. We also let parents eat with their kids once a month. Having parents see you working the cafeteria will pay dividends well into the future. Chicken Chunk Surprise for everyone!

Holding monthly "coffee with the principal" meetings is a great way to bring your school community together. Keep the agenda light with the focus on coming together to build a shared vision. These coffees are a great time to bring in a guest speaker to talk about prevalent issues in the community or to introduce parents to new support structures. Even if there is no agenda, parents will appreciate the fact that you are there to interface with them. One idea to keep in mind is to hold one coffee in the morning and then the next one in the afternoon in order to accommodate parents with different work schedules.

A well-planned "coffee with the principal" promotion is essential to making it a success. Send a notice home with students or post it on the school's website or social media accounts. The notice should include the date, time, location, and purpose of the meeting, as well as any other relevant information or instructions. Use an automated phone message as a quick and effective way to reach parents with the information. Make sure to keep the message brief and clear, and provide a callback number or website for more information. If your school community speaks a language other than English, ensure that your message is translated.

Most schools will use email to communicate with parents. Send a reminder a few days before the meeting with all the details, including any agenda items, and encourage them to attend. In addition, social media can be a great way to reach a wide audience quickly. Consider creating a Facebook event or posting updates on Twitter or Instagram to promote the meeting. Lastly, creating posters and flyers and distributing them around the school or community, such as in local businesses, libraries, and community centers, can be a great way to increase visibility and get more stakeholders involved.

Visibility also includes doing the work that would generally be outside the scope of the job description of a principal. As you will discover, being a principal means that you need to be a jack-of-all-trades. For example, just a few weeks into my tenure as an elementary school principal, I was getting ready for my first Back-to-School night. I realized that the table supporting my LCD projector was too short and caused the image on the screen to be distorted. I needed a taller table, and fast. The evening was about to begin and the auditorium was full of parents. I went to the back of the auditorium and picked up a table, hoisted it over my head and walked down the aisle and placed it in the front of the auditorium. As I did this, I overheard several parents saying, "Now there's a principal that takes charge." All I was doing was carrying a table.

Another example of this notion comes from the times our school flooded. The playground was next to a river that would flood when there were several days of heavy rain in a row. Several times in the five years I was there, the blacktop flooded and was underwater. While we waited for water trucks to clear out the debris and mud, I would go out there in rain boots and use a wide industrial broom to try to clear out as much as I could. Looking back, I was never able to clear out much, but it was the fact that I tried that was important. Our students couldn't use the blacktop at recess until it was cleared. The school community saw me out there, doing my best to get recess up and running again.

One of the most focused-on aspects of being visible is, you guessed it, what do you wear? This is a tricky question. I am not a fan of spending energy creating a work dress code for teachers and staff members. There is a very passionate and very real debate among educators over whether or not to allow teachers to wear jeans to work. In my opinion, we have more pressing issues to worry about.

As far as what principals should wear, that is a little bit different. As a teacher, I wore combinations of button-down shirts and khaki pants, polos and jeans, and sometimes a sport coat or sweater. As a young teacher, I knew I had to look professional every day.

If I came to work wearing a T-shirt and an old pair of jeans, I would look less like a teacher or more like someone who was headed to the coffee shop. As a new principal in my late twenties, my notion of what I should wear didn't change much. Over time, I started to wear more school spirit shirts. I wanted to be comfortable and able to be competitive on the basketball court with my students.

One thing to consider is your geography. I have visited schools in the Southwest where every day is polo shirt day. When you are dealing with 100-degree temperatures, you need to adapt. I have seen principals on the West Coast dress more casually than their East Coast counterparts. School leaders in the South seem to take professional dress to the next level, with bow ties and jackets.

At the end of the day, dress for the role and the work you are engaged in. Walking around the campus all day every day made me switch from dress shoes to tennis shoes. I have worked with many female principals who keep a variety of shoes in their office. Look at what your colleagues in your district are wearing. My advice would be to figure out who is dressed somewhere in the middle of formal and informal and wear something a touch more formal than what they are wearing. This is especially true in your first year when you are trying to establish yourself in your district.

What Now?

Being seen is one of the easiest elements to employ, but can be one of the most difficult to execute. Finding the time amidst the 50,000 things that come up throughout the day to be outside with kids, parents, and teachers can be an unexpected challenge. Here's how to get it done:

1. Schedule these visible moments. Put them on your calendar. Have the courage to tell people that you can't talk right now because you have an important engagement to attend to.
2. Dismissal in the rain is one of the worst parts of working at a school. However, it is a great way for parents to see your

dedication to the kids and the school by ensuring that the pickup line is moving smoothly even in inclement weather. Getting soaked and being cold and wet for a short amount of time will get you a lot of brownie points.

3. Reach out to a few of your more active parents and have them plan your first "coffee with the principal." This will ensure that it will get planned, as this is an activity that is easy to let fall through the cracks. Have these parents also invite a couple of their friends. This way, you can ensure that you are starting off with a friendly and engaged group of parents.

Chapter 6
Professional Learning Communities (PLCs)

Professional Learning Communities (PLCs) can change the culture of a school. In order to accomplish this, however, a strong, competent leader must guide the way. Many schools claim to have productive and comprehensive PLCs that are centered around teaching and learning. However, most of these schools are only scratching the surface when it comes to true collaboration and creating a student-centered approach. Without the right guidance, PLCs are just meetings renamed to seem more purposeful. This can lead to further frustration, stagnation, and disengagement. There are several elements that must be in place for any PLC to be successful and purposeful.

Warwas and Helm (2018) showed that the high presence of PLCs contributes to the creation of a stimulating learning environment. Existing evidence also indicates that participation in PLCs stimulates the use of effective instructional strategies. For example, Wahlstrom and Louis (2008) found that the dimensions of PLCs are positively linked to teachers promoting students' engagement, successful use of instructional time, and differentiation of instruction. Some researchers (Doğan, Pringle, & Mesa, 2016; Vanblaere & Devos, 2018) reported that teacher involvement in PLCs is positively associated with changes in their practice. The characteristics of PLCs are positive predictors of the self-efficacy of novice teachers (De Neve, Devos, & Tuytens, 2015). Finally, meta-analytical findings (Lomos, Hofman, & Bosker, 2011) indicate that there are statistically significant effects of PLCs on student achievement.

It is vital that educators get comfortable with team norms. Educators are usually comfortable creating rules and expectations for their classrooms. However, they get a bit reluctant to create norms for themselves and their colleagues. Principals must ensure that this important step is not overlooked. Every PLC must start with norms to ensure that all members are working toward common goals and to keep student learning at the forefront of every conversation. PLC members also should not be afraid to stop discussions and call out when a norm has been broken. This shift beyond collegiality is vital. Principals need to create an environment where teachers are comfortable in discussing the uncomfortable. It is important that everyone can speak clinically about the data, but not critically. This is where PLCs break down.

I have always liked the idea of posting group norms in a public place at the school for all to see. This helps to further instill a collaborative culture. Remember, the principal is also the Chief Culture Officer.

Always remember, PLC Time Is Sacred. Teacher time is often gobbled up by miscellaneous staff meetings, parent conferences, and putting out fires. For PLCs to be successful and meaningful, principals must protect PLC time at all costs. Teachers should never be pulled from PLCs unless it is an emergency. If teachers are constantly pulled from their PLC time, the work that is put in will be in jeopardy and there is a risk that the ongoing work of a PLC will be seen as frivolous. In addition, all educators must be held accountable for participating in collaboration.

Principals can create either physical binders or electronic folders to house meeting agendas, student assessment data, next steps, and research on best practices. These binders or folders should be accessible by everyone at the school site. Transparency is important. What is happening in one grade level or department should not be a secret to everyone else. Many teachers have worked a variety of grade levels or subject areas in their career. By giving them access to other PLCs' work, they can possibly bring a new perspective to an issue and help to problem solve a situation.

The PLC process must be defined. Educators should never be thrown into the PLC world without a clearly defined process. While educator teams need parameters to work within, they also need to be free to customize the process to meet their needs. While principals should give teachers space to explore these steps on their own with their PLC, they should also set up teacher teams for success by guiding them through the process. A sample process for instruction and data analysis is as follows:

- Unpack Standards
  - Doing this will aid teachers in the planning of instruction for the upcoming unit.
- Identify POWER Standards for the Unit
  - These standards are the most prevalent in the unit as well as the most represented in the overall grade level.
- Create Scales and Rubrics to Define Progress
  - Assessing student understanding should be uniform in nature. A teacher should be using a clear set of rubrics and scales to determine where a student is on the learning continuum.
- Design Common Formative Assessments
  - Two sixth-grade math teachers should be assessing their students using the same assessment in order to compare the results with their PLC. That way, they are comparing apples to apples, not apples to chicken nuggets.
- Process Check
  - Creating rubrics/scales and common formative assessments need to be completed BEFORE instruction begins!
- Design Instruction
  - Instructional plans should not be created in isolation. While all teachers are unique and have different styles, it is vital to ensure that instructional delivery includes the same academic elements in the unit.

- Gather Data/Analyze Results
  - Teachers need to gather several data points in order to ensure that the data is valid. Too often, educators only use a summative assessment. It is important that we assess for learning along the way, not just create assessments of learning at the end.
- Remediate or Enrich Learning
  - Assessment data is useless unless you do something with it. Teachers need to ask themselves and their team to determine next steps. Is remediation in order or can students go deeper into the content?
- Teacher Reflection on Instructional Practices and Results
  - This part is the hardest and explains why principals need to ensure a clinical and not critical environment. Teachers need to be honest with themselves on what worked, what didn't work, and what they can do differently next time.

PLC team roles must be clearly defined to keep discussions focused on student learning as well as to ensure accountability at every level of the team. Having roles also will keep team members engaged. Sample team roles could be facilitator, recorder, time-keeper, and reporter.

- Facilitator: Develops agenda, runs the meeting, keeps team focused, and ensures equity of voice throughout the team
- Recorder: Takes meeting minutes, posts minutes in PLC binder or in shared online drive, maintains data binder or online database
- Timekeeper: Monitors agenda items and keeps meeting flowing, keeps track of start and end times, discerns the need to table an item or to make a decision based on time
- Reporter: Reviews norms at the beginning of the meeting, ensures that norms are followed, reviews previous minutes before the meeting begins, acts as a liaison between the PLC and school leadership

Team roles can change monthly, quarterly, or yearly, depending on the desires of the school as a whole. It is important that everyone on the PLC team serve time in one of these roles in order to ensure accountability.

In order for PLCs to be highly functional teams, educators must move beyond collegiality and not be afraid to engage in discourse. It is advisable that team members disagree with ideas, not people. This helps everyone to be clinical, not critical, in difficult situations. This is important also when looking at data. If students are not performing well, PLC teams must address the real issues and not sugarcoat potential instructional concerns. We are not doing students any favors by looking the other way when we know something needs to be addressed. Always being "nice" can prevent the true change needed to move a school forward.

What Now?

Creating working PLCs takes time. Don't rush the process. Get started on the right foot with these ideas:

1. Take your leadership team to visit a school with strong PLCs. There is nothing quite as powerful as seeing the PLC process in action. When starting from scratch, it will be helpful for teachers to experience the conversations, the support, and the data analysis of a comprehensive PLC.
2. Educate your teachers and parents about PLCs. Parents need to understand that your teachers will be going on a new journey. By having them understand the process, it will help keep the school accountable.
3. Ask the right questions. One of the main components of PLCs is asking these four essential questions: (1) What do we want students to know? (2) How will we know they have learned it? (3) What would we do if they didn't learn it? (4) What would we do if they did learn it? Start using these questions in your daily conversations with teachers. It is important to get your staff thinking in these terms.

Chapter 7
Looking at the Right Data

School leadership teams spend hours and hours each school year looking at assessment data. Data will help teachers and administrators target individual students and standards for intervention. However, assessment data is only part of the picture. There is a wide variety of data out there that needs to be analyzed in order to truly transform schools and to change student outcomes. Unfortunately, most leadership teams never move beyond assessment data.

The *Hechinger Report*, a national nonprofit newsroom, writes "What good data can do is provide educators with more evidence and focus as they create instructional plans that are responsive to the needs of each student. . . Data should have a purpose and an impact: How do you intend to use it to support more effective instruction? What do you need to change, and how will you measure that it's working? In between, you have meaningful analysis" (Minnich, 2022).

Following are five pieces of data your leadership teams should be analyzing:

Attendance Data

It doesn't matter how great the teachers are, or how engaging the content is. You can spend thousands of dollars on hands-on activities, field trips, and educational technology. None of these things will make a difference if students are not at school.

Let me repeat that. None of these things will make a difference if students are not at school.

I'll pass along a great piece of advice I received from another principal as I was just getting started in my administrative career. He told me, "The number-one job of a principal is to get butts in seats. If you can get butts in seats, you can then start to work on everything else."

Students with poor attendance need an intervention. Parents meetings must be set up and attendance plans created. Home visits can be very powerful for students who are truant. We will talk more about student attendance in a later chapter.

Discipline Data

Most school data systems have a place for discipline tracking. It is important that infractions are tracked in order to provide students with behavioral interventions. However, I have always found it interesting to see where the infractions were coming from. By analyzing this data by teacher, or by grade level, you might be able to see an area of opportunity with classroom management training. Behavioral issues at your school might not be solely a student issue as many teachers struggle with classroom management.

Try this: Create a graphical representation of the disciplinary data at your school. Specifically, indicate the number of times students are sent to the office by individual teachers. Be sure you remove the names of the teachers! Remember, we look at data clinically, not critically. The results might be shocking to both you and your staff as sometimes the vast majority of office referrals come from just a handful of classrooms.

Instructional Minutes

By instructional minutes, I don't mean how many minutes of the day students are at school. By instructional minutes, I do mean tracking how many minutes students are actually engaged in learning. When I first became a principal, I conducted classroom observations and kept track of how long students were engaged in active learning.

The average engagement time was 11 minutes per 52-minute period. We defined active learning as anytime students were speaking with each other, working on a hands-on project, or participating in a discussion or group work. It was eye opening to see how much time students were sitting in class, passively listening to the teacher, reading silently, or completing an independent worksheet.

Special Education

We need to look at Special Education as an intervention, not a forever program. Some students, depending on their disability, might require Special Education services for their entire academic lives. However, most students should be able to move in-between programs and eventually be exited. This should be the goal of every IEP. This is especially true for students receiving OT, Speech, and PT services. Keep track of the number of students who are entering and exiting these programs.

English Language Learner Reclassification

The goal of all English Language Development (ELD) programs is to ensure that students are proficient in English. Students can be reclassified and designated as fluent beginning in second grade. It is this data point that will enable a leadership team to gauge the impact of ELD programs. We should not deem a program successful at a school site if students are not being reclassified. Long-term ELD students should also be a data point to consider. It is troublesome to note that some schools have students on their rosters who have been receiving ELD support for over six years without being reclassified.

What Now?

Data collection is a fundamental step in the PLC process as well as overall school improvement. This element is critical to the success of the school. Start your data analysis process by addressing the following:

1. Identify a method to collect data. While many schools have a School Information System (SIS) that can easily pull out attendance and academic data, it gets a little more tricky when it comes to discipline, reclassification, and Special Education data. In most cases, this data will be collected from a variety of sources. Bring all of these data points together.
2. Having the right data can help educators find the root cause of the problem. When addressing concerns with teachers, always use data to conduct your analysis.
3. Have your data easily accessible during meetings with one teacher or all of your teachers at once. It is important that teachers get into the habit of bringing data to meetings and referring to it rather than using speculation. Modeling this notion will help set the expectation.

Tales from the Principal's Desk

B eing a principal is hard work. No one understands the role until they are in it. Over the past several decades, the principal's role has changed from described as a manager of sorts to an instructional leader. While being a competent teacher and understanding pedagogy is important, knowing how to lead others toward a common goal should be the apex of your work. While it can be tempting and familiar to focus on instruction, a principal needs to focus on leadership.

As a new principal, I was very unsure of myself. I was working with teachers that were twice my age with double the amount of experience. Our state test scores were in the bottom 25%. Our students were performing poorly on our local assessments. We were dealing with sizable discipline issues and a parent community that was disengaged (or uninterested, according to many teachers). After conducting dozens of instructional rounds, I could tell that the actual instruction in classrooms could be vastly improved. However, I knew that if I tried to discuss instructional practices with them, I would be caught between a rock and a hard place, as I did not have enough experience in their eyes to do so. I had to focus on something more tangible – data.

Data can be cold and unemotional. Data doesn't care who is looking at them. Numbers are numbers. They don't change in the moment and give you a snapshot of a point in time.

I dove into the achievement data of our students, but it was hard to determine the best place to start as it all looked pretty dismal. Teachers had told me that they had tried every academic intervention strategy under the sun. It was difficult to figure out where to begin.

That's when I noticed something . . .

Our poorest performing students were the same students who had high truancy rates and made frequent trips to the office on disciplinary referrals. We were focusing on the wrong data.

The best instruction, the best academic interventions, the best social-emotional learning programs don't mean anything unless kids are in school. It was time to get butts in seats.

We created a brand-new attendance plan for the school. The front office spent the first part of each day tracking down students who were absent. We wanted to know why students were not at school. If we couldn't reach families by phone, we initiated a home visit the following day. Spanish was the prevalent language in the community I worked in. For home visits, I brought along my community liaison, who not only translated for me but also knew many of our families on a personal basis. For our more severe cases, I brought our Student Resource Officer (SRO), not as a scare tactic, but as a support for parents struggling to get their challenging children to school.

Any student who was late to a class throughout the day had an automated call sent home to parents. We were relentless and shared our goals with our community often in order to get their buy-in as well as provide regular updates. We even posted grade-level attendance rates in our monthly newsletter.

One important aspect of our plan was that if a parent called in a child absent for being ill from time to time, we did not employ our resources in the same way. We wanted our students who were ill to stay home and get better quickly so that they could return to school quickly.

The result . . .

Our average daily attendance rate went from 92% to 98% in one year. But that was just the starting point. Now that we had "butts in seats" we could focus on other aspects of our data. What we weren't counting on was that better attendance was the driver for everything else that followed.

Because students were in class more often, they missed out on less instruction. That meant they didn't fall as far behind academically or feel as lost as in previous years. Teachers saw an immediate improvement in student engagement, leading to fewer disciplinary issues. When issues did come up, we dealt with them with parents as partners, being transparent about our disciplinary matrix. We again used our SROs to act as supports, providing families with community resources to get further assistance.

With attendance rates up and discipline rates down, we could then focus on instruction. We wanted to ensure that teachers were providing students with the best instruction possible during the time they were at school; however, we focused less on quantity of instruction and spent more time on content and how we were providing instruction. In the past, teachers voiced concern over not having enough time to teach due to student disruptions and student absences. I knew I needed to collect some data on instruction time and how it was spent each class period.

I took a week and sat in at least one class period for every teacher on campus. I tracked how much actual teacher-directed instruction was taking place. I kept track of lost minutes during transitions, student disruptions, and individual seat work on worksheets that seemed more like busywork than anything else. I was shocked by what I found. On average, students were engaged in learning only 11 minutes out of a 54-minute period.

I knew that our students were bored, disengaged, and disinterested. Now I knew why.

With two important issues under control, discipline and attendance, we turned our attention to increasing student engagement with project-based learning, inquiry-based learning, and hands-on experiences. I deployed our instructional coach to work with our struggling teachers to provide them with different engagement strategies. We also spent a lot of time with our new teachers. Our school and district as a whole had a high attrition rate when it came to teachers. We knew that our success as a school relied not only on our new teachers being successful, but also on their sticking around to continue to positively impact our culture.

We also dove into Professional Learning Communities. We had to get comfortable with acknowledging our strengths and our weaknesses, and with asking for help. Our school was extremely siloed. We reimagined staff meeting time into PLC time where each week, teachers would look at student data, reflect upon their own instruction, and create common formative assessments together.

Don't get me wrong, there were tears. Lots of tears. We had to conduct some deep reflection in order to be able to move forward. Don't rush this process. It might take weeks. Let it happen. Don't be afraid of the storm. Blue skies will come.

Questions to Ask Yourself:

- Am I fostering a positive and inclusive school culture? Reflect on your ability to create a welcoming and inclusive environment where all students, teachers, and staff feel valued, respected, and supported. Consider how your leadership practices promote collaboration, open communication, and a sense of belonging among stakeholders. Assess whether you are actively addressing issues of equity, diversity, and cultural responsiveness within the school community.
- Am I effectively supporting and developing my teachers and staff? Evaluate how well you are supporting the professional growth and well-being of your teachers and staff. Consider whether you are providing meaningful professional development opportunities, coaching, and mentoring to help them thrive in their roles. Reflect on your ability to cultivate a positive working environment that encourages teamwork, innovation,

and continuous learning. Assess how well you are fostering a sense of empowerment and agency among your staff.

- Am I leading with a clear vision and strategic direction? Reflect on your ability to articulate a clear vision for the school and effectively communicate that vision to the entire school community. Assess whether you are providing a compelling and inspiring direction that aligns with the needs and aspirations of your students, teachers, and community. Consider how well you are developing and implementing strategic plans to achieve the vision, and whether you are monitoring progress and adjusting strategies as needed.

Pillar II

Instruction

Chapter 8

Instruction Matters

Good instruction matters. Actually, it more than matters. How instruction is delivered can either light a spark that lasts a lifetime and inspires the child to learn more, or it can lead to frustration and reluctance to learn more.

I never considered myself a master teacher. I could never clearly articulate complex instructional theories or methods. Out of all of the conferences from around the country that I have spoken at, not once did I speak on the topic of instruction.

When I was a middle school music teacher, my administrators never brought a new teacher to my room to observe my masterful instructional prowess. I was never asked to mentor a new teacher who was struggling to give high-level instruction. From my point of view, staff meetings and professional development centered around instructional strategies were optional.

As I considered a transition from the classroom to the front office, I wasn't worried about my ability to connect with students, my skills in student engagement and classroom management, or my strengths in bringing parents and community members into the school. I was, however, worried that this self-admitted lack of traditional classroom instruction experience would cause teachers not to trust me. Most of the principals whom I knew were former core classroom teachers: English/language arts, math, multiple subjects always dominated the field. They also had more than five years of experience as a teacher, with many of them serving in several school districts working in diverse communities. I was coming from a middle school in an upper-middle-class beach community in California as a music teacher. I never had my *Stand and Deliver* moment, my "Oh Captain, my captain" awakening, or my Freedom Writers breakthrough. However, I was probably one of the only music teachers to have students perform a traditional classical piece, followed by "Crazy Train" by Ozzy Osbourne, and then finish it off with the main theme from *Star Wars*.

The path from music teacher to principal was not one frequently traveled.

I felt this much more when I became an elementary school principal than when I was at the middle school level. When I arrived on campus, I felt that I was immediately being sized up. Everyone knew that I was coming from the middle school setting. There were many questions about my experience, or lack thereof, with younger students. Did I understand what eight-year-olds were capable of? Could I support teachers with academic intervention ideas and curriculum adoptions? Did I know how to teach a first grader to read? Would I be able to handle whatever happens in kindergarten? Well, to be fair, most of us aren't prepared for what goes on in a kindergarten classroom.

Looking back now, I was in way over my head at the beginning. We all have heard the phrase "Fake it till you make it." I'll be honest, I was faking it at the beginning. However, the more I listened, observed, and experienced, the more confident I became in my abilities as a school leader.

However, I came out the other side five years later with a Principal of the Year award; our school was the highest-ranked in the district when it came to culture, as voted on by teachers and parents; our school received the prestigious California Distinguished School Award for the first time in its history.

What Now?

I have never liked the idea that principals have to be instructional experts. Yes, they need to be strong teachers, but not necessarily members of the Teacher Hall of Fame. Secondary principals typically hold single-subject credentials and taught one subject in their career. Elementary teachers who become elementary principals will have a more aligned work experience than their secondary counterparts. If you are feeling out of your element, here are a few ways to get started on your instructional leadership journey.

1. Own your journey. I was never going to be able to convince anyone that I knew more about teaching 5- and 6-year-olds than the kindergarten teachers. Own what you do know and acknowledge what you don't know. Your staff will respect you for it.
2. Know your strengths. You were chosen for this position for a reason. Don't forget that. Chances are, there were dozens of applicants who applied to the position who were 100% qualified. However, you are the one taking on the role of the principal, not them.
3. Get uncomfortable with being comfortable. This is a hard job and not for everyone. Understand that it is going to be tough.

Chapter 9

It's Not How Much Time, but What You Do with It

Children spend around 8 hours a day at school about 180 days per year. On average, students spend about 6.5 hours per day with theory teacher(s). In total, primary students are with their teacher for around 1,170 hours or 49 full days per year. Secondary students are with individual teachers for around 7 total days per year. In total, students are in school an average of 64,800 minutes per year. Just by looking at the numbers, it is without question that a teacher can make a huge impact on the life of a child.

Think about it: 49 days per year in elementary school.

A teacher with that much time with their students can truly create a learning atmosphere of excitement, wonder, and collaboration, as well as instill a lifelong love of learning. Kids are coming home from school bursting with excitement to tell their parents about what they did in school that day. That excitement leads to further exploration with the whole family in the form of trips to the zoo, a museum, the beach, the mountains, or to the park down the street. The child's room becomes a research facility on ancient Egypt, or a lab for testing new theories and compounds.

Yes, it gets messy. But that's what life as a child is all about.

Sadly, the opposite is also true. Children who are in classrooms that do not inspire creativity, teamwork, and exploration will not only miss out on deep levels of learning, but also not experience the joy of learning in a fun and creative way.

There is a question that haunts the lives of teachers everywhere: "Why do we have to learn this?" I have found that students who have inspiring teachers ask this question far less often than those who have a teacher who is dry, predictable, and, well, boring.

Teachers can explain how the concepts they are teaching are applicable in real-life situations. For example, if teaching algebra, the teacher can explain how algebra is used. Teachers can also explain how the concepts they are teaching are relevant to the student's future education or career goals. For example, if teaching history, the teacher can explain how understanding historical events and movements can help students understand current events and societal issues.

Connecting how learning the material will help students build critical thinking, problem-solving, and analytical skills that will be invaluable throughout their lives, not just in the immediate future. Teachers can ask students what they are interested in and then connect the lesson to their interests. If a student is interested in sports, the teacher can explain how learning physics concepts can help them understand the mechanics of a basketball shot or the forces involved in a soccer kick.

Teachers can encourage students to explore and discover new information and ideas for themselves. By fostering curiosity and a love of learning, students will be more motivated to learn and less likely to ask, "Why do we have to learn this?" in the first place.

Remember, 49 days in elementary, 7 days in secondary.

Every year, most districts ask their principals to add up instructional minutes to submit to the school board to show that the school not only meets the state's instructional minutes requirements, but adheres to local policy as well. You will spend hours calculating and adding up minutes for regular school days, minimum days, half days, and any other days that you might have. It is truly a mind-numbing activity that has zero bearing on educational outcomes.

Think about learning a new language. On the surface, one could argue that learning can be equated to the amount of time spent on studying the new language. However, it is more than just that. It is about how the person is learning the new language and what tools they are using to make the learning more meaningful.

While school leadership matters, it is what happens in the classroom that makes all the difference. One of the biggest mistakes that principals make is assuming they have to be master teachers. This way of thinking must be shifted to principals being able to support master teachers and provide them the environment they need to be successful. In addition, principals also need to understand what types of support new teachers need. But that doesn't mean that the principal will always be providing those supports.

Principals can provide instructional leadership by setting clear expectations for teaching and learning, modeling effective instructional practices, and facilitating professional development opportunities for teachers. School leaders can encourage collaboration among teachers by providing opportunities for them to work together on curriculum development, instructional strategies, and assessments. By promoting a culture of collaboration, principals can help ensure that all teachers are aligned in their teaching practices and working toward the same goals.

Principals need to monitor student progress through data analysis, classroom observations, and teacher feedback. By tracking student progress, principals can identify areas where teachers may need additional support or resources and adjust instructional strategies as needed. In addition, school leaders can provide teachers with the resources and support they need to be effective in the classroom, including access to technology, instructional materials, and professional development opportunities. By communicating with families about school goals and instructional practices, principals can build trust and promote engagement in the learning process.

Expert teacher instruction is important for several reasons. When teachers plan and deliver effective instruction, students are more likely to retain and apply the knowledge and skills they acquire. Teachers who use a variety of teaching strategies, provide clear explanations, give constructive feedback, and actively involve students in the learning process can help to create a positive and stimulating learning environment that encourages students to engage with the material and achieve better learning outcomes. Moreover, good teacher instruction can increase student engagement and motivation, making learning more enjoyable and meaningful for students.

Secondly, strong teacher instruction is important for the development of students' critical thinking and problem-solving skills. Teachers who use inquiry-based instruction, collaborative learning, and project-based learning approaches can help students to develop these skills. By encouraging students to think deeply about the material and apply their knowledge in real-world contexts, teachers can help students develop into effective problem solvers and independent thinkers.

In today's rapidly changing and competitive job market, it is essential for students to develop skills that will help them succeed in the workplace. One such skill is communication, which is crucial in any workplace. In school, students need to learn to communicate effectively through writing, public speaking, and interpersonal communication. They can also learn to listen actively and respond appropriately to feedback, which is important for building positive relationships with coworkers and supervisors.

Another important skill is collaboration. The ability to work effectively with others is a critical skill in today's team-oriented workplace. Students need to work collaboratively through group projects, debates, and other collaborative learning activities. They can learn to contribute their own ideas, listen to others' ideas, and work together to achieve common goals.

Students need to have the opportunity to practice these skills in classrooms in order to be best prepared for their futures. They will not learn these skills by completing a worksheet by themselves in silence.

"You've probably heard of the 10,000-hour rule, which was popularized by Malcolm Gladwell's blockbuster book *Outliers*. As Gladwell tells it, the rule goes like this: it takes 10,000 hours of intensive practice to achieve mastery of complex skills and materials, like playing the violin or getting as good as Bill Gates at computer programming.

"Gladwell describes one central study in particular, about which he writes, 'their research suggests that once a musician has enough ability to get into a top music school, the thing that distinguishes one performer from another is how hard he or she works. That's it'" (Young, 2020).

But that's not it, according to the researchers. It's a bit more complicated when you dig into it.

And it turns out his study shows that there's another important variable that Gladwell doesn't focus on: how good a student's teacher is.

Practice is important, and it's surprising how much it takes to master something complicated. Research suggests that someone could practice for thousands of hours and still not be a master performer. They could be outplayed by someone who practiced less but had a teacher who showed them just what to focus on at a key moment in their practice regimen (Young, 2020).

What Now?

Many new principals are surprised with the heavy focus on accounting for every instruction minute during the year. Focus your time on making those minutes count. Here are some ideas to get you started.

1. Get into classrooms. Get into classrooms often. It is vital that you know what is going on in your classrooms.
2. Track transition time. In many instances, instructional time is lost due to poor transitions. Help your teachers make these transitions smoother and more efficient.
3. Understand what your students are doing in class. Is it a lot of seat work or are students collaborating together? What are their actions? What are the intended outcomes?

Chapter 10
Shifting from Teacher-Led to Teacher-Facilitated Instruction

I remember the day that my father brought home our first computer. It was an IBM. It weighed a ton, had a very small monitor, and was a creamy, yellow-brown color. It took forever to boot up and could only do a few things. I used our family computer throughout my childhood to write papers, play educational games, and in high school, begin to explore the internet. I have distinct memories of my parents taking me to our public library so that I could check out books to research and to cite in my projects.

One of the most frustrating memories from this area of my childhood was asking my parents for help or for an answer to a question. Their common response was "Look it up." That drove me crazy. Even worse was when I asked them how to spell something. I was, and am, a notoriously bad speller.

"Look it up."

As a child of the 1980s and early 1990s, I thought my teachers knew everything. Maybe they did. Maybe they didn't. But I thought they did. If I asked a question, they either knew the answer, or knew where to find the answer.

They were the gatekeepers of my education. Other than going to the public library, there was nowhere else I could quickly or easily turn to learn more about the topic we were discussing in class.

Fast-forward to today, my own children can Google the answer to how far Neptune is from Earth, ask Alexa what the temperature is in Santiago, Chile, and catch up with their favorite celebrities of TikTok, Instagram, and Facebook. Kids across the world can now attend school online, without a live teacher, from their bedrooms. In the eyes of a child, the physical walls of a school no longer hold all the knowledge in the world. It's available from a few keystrokes or by simply saying, "Alexa" or "Siri."

Teacher-led instruction looks and feels like it has for decades. The teacher is always in front of the classroom, desks are in straight rows, students are quietly listening to the teacher, or staring off into space in the direction of the teacher. New material is often introduced on a Monday, a quiz is taken on Wednesday, and the test is on Friday. The next week is the same. And the next. And the next.

Wash. Rinse. Repeat.

As an education system, schools need to switch from teacher-led to teacher-facilitated instruction. Teachers are no longer the gatekeepers of information, but are instrumental in teaching students how to digest the information and apply it to real-world situations.

School leaders need to lead discussions and movements that embrace a student-led approach. A good place to begin is to redesign physical and virtual learning spaces to support student-centered approaches. This may involve creating flexible classrooms that accommodate collaborative group work, independent study areas, and access to technology resources. In addition, schools can develop virtual platforms or learning management systems that facilitate personalized learning and student collaboration.

Creating a variety of seating options that allow students to choose what works best for their learning preferences can yield powerful results. This can include bean bags, standing desks, floor cushions, or movable furniture. Flexible seating arrangements can promote collaboration, comfort, and independence.

Designate different areas within the classroom for specific activities or learning experiences. For example, create a reading nook with a cozy seating area, a maker space for hands-on projects, or a technology corner with devices and charging stations. These dedicated learning zones help students engage in different types of activities and allow for more personalized and self-directed learning.

Teachers and office staff should encourage students to contribute to the school and classroom environment by displaying their artwork, writing samples, or collaborative projects. This not only celebrates their achievements but also creates a visually stimulating and inspiring learning environment.

Redesigning learning spaces can also involve designating areas (or providing mobile carts) with materials for students to engage in creative and innovative activities. This can include art supplies, STEM materials, building blocks, or digital tools for multimedia creation. Having dedicated spaces for creativity and innovation allows students to explore their interests and engage in hands-on learning experiences.

Collaborative workspaces are an important aspect of a student-led environment. These spaces can include round tables, whiteboards or chalkboards for brainstorming, and accessible materials for group projects. Designing collaborative workspaces encourages teamwork, communication, and problem-solving skills among students.

Weather depending, schools can utilize outdoor spaces, such as courtyards or gardens, to provide opportunities for hands-on learning, exploration, and nature-based experiences. Schools can set up seating areas or workstations where students can engage in outdoor projects, observations, or group discussions. Outdoor learning spaces promote environmental awareness, physical activity, and a connection to the natural world.

Schools should prioritize giving students a voice in their learning by involving them in the decision-making process. This can be achieved through activities such as student-led conferences, student councils, or surveys to gather feedback and suggestions. By valuing student perspectives and involving them in shaping their learning experiences, schools empower students to take ownership of their education.

Principals need to establish a safe, inclusive, and supportive environment that encourages risk-taking, collaboration, and creativity among staff and students. This includes promoting a growth mindset among students, fostering positive relationships between students and teachers, and establishing norms and expectations that support student-centered learning. In addition, schools should actively involve parents and the community in supporting student-centered approaches. This can be achieved through regular communication, parent workshops, and community partnerships that promote real-world connections and provide opportunities for students to engage in authentic learning experiences.

Implementing a student-centered approach requires a commitment from all stakeholders and a willingness to embrace innovative practices. By creating a shared vision, providing professional development, redesigning learning spaces, fostering student agency, utilizing formative assessment, cultivating a supportive environment, and engaging parents and the community, schools can successfully transition to a student-centered approach that prioritizes the unique needs and interests of each learner.

In the past, group projects, project-based learning, choice activities, and utilizing technology were considered "special" and out of the ordinary. In today's educational landscape, principals must encourage this shift and give teachers the license to be more creative, more diverse in their instructional approaches, and use varied assessments to gauge mastery.

Group projects give students the opportunity to work from their strengths and to build important skills such as collaboration, communication, and to develop problem-solving skills. The vast majority of students in schools will go on to careers where they will have to work with others in order to complete tasks and projects. They need to learn those skills in school. By working together, students increase their information-gathering potential. Students are no longer limited to using the books found in the library, but now have access to a vast amount of information online. This should be encouraged and celebrated.

Project-based learning (PBL) gives students the chance to work with their peers to solve a problem. PBL is an instructional approach in which students actively engage in real-world or simulated problems or challenges. In this process, students investigate, design, create, and present solutions to complex, multifaceted problems. The group becomes both teacher and student, with everyone contributing to the conversation and learning from each other.

Examples of PBL projects include designing a sustainable community, creating a business plan, conducting scientific research, producing a short film, or organizing a community service event. Principals need to support these types of projects both in funding and in resources.

Choice activities allow students the freedom to "choose their own adventure." In reality, however, in most situations students will pick from predetermined choices. Nevertheless, the freedom of choice adds to the notion of autonomy and independence in the classroom. Choice activities also allow students to work on a topic that interests them. This will lead to increased engagement, decreased levels of classroom disruption, as well as deeper knowledge retention.

Choice activities can take many forms, including:

1. Choice boards: These are grids that provide a set of activities or tasks for students to choose from, each with a different level of complexity or difficulty.
2. Menu options: These are a set of options presented to students, such as creating a presentation, writing an essay, or making a poster.
3. Interest-based projects: These allow students to choose a topic that they are interested in and create a project on that topic.

The benefits of choice activities in education are numerous. It allows students to engage in learning that is meaningful to them and increases their motivation and engagement in the classroom. It also provides opportunities for differentiation, where students can choose activities that align with their interests, strengths, and learning styles. In addition, it helps to develop decision-making skills and fosters a sense of responsibility and ownership in their learning process.

A meta-analysis of 20 years of research synthesized the quantitative results, comparing the effects of PBL and traditional instruction on students' academic achievement and studies in a variety of educational settings. The findings present a quantitative ES estimate (0.71) based on individual studies, i.e. a medium to large and positive effect on student academic achievement in PBL compared with traditional instruction, providing reliable evidence that PBL is much more effective than traditional instruction with regard to enhancing students' academic achievement (Chen & Yang, 2019).

Active learning and passive learning are two contrasting approaches. Passive learning refers to an antiquated classroom model where the teacher lectures while students take notes and listen passively. In passive learning, students are not actively engaged in the learning process, and the teacher is the primary source of knowledge. Passive learning can be effective in some contexts, but it does not promote critical thinking, problem-solving, or creativity. Students in passive learning environments may struggle to retain information long-term, and they may not be able to apply what they have learned to new situations.

You want to avoid the passive learning environment at all costs. This is an out-of-date model of instruction that does not benefit students in today's education environment.

Active learning, on the other hand, is a more student-centered approach to learning. Active learning involves students in the learning process through hands-on activities, group discussions, problem-solving exercises, and other interactive learning experiences. In active learning, students are encouraged to ask questions, explore ideas, and apply what they have learned in practical contexts. Active learning is highly effective in promoting student engagement, motivation, and critical thinking. Students who engage in active learning are more likely to retain information, apply what they have learned, and develop skills that are essential for success in the twenty-first-century workforce.

A word of caution. Active classrooms are noisy and busy, with students up and out of their seats, working with others, and using the room as they need. The pushback you will receive is that students can't handle being productive in this type of environment. This is just a deflection point as reluctant teachers do not want to give up their self-perceived sense of control in the classroom.

Teacher-directed classrooms all look the same. The teacher's desk is in the front of the classroom, either in the center or just to the side of the board. Desks are in columns and rows. I like to call this cemetery seating, because it resembles how graves are distributed in a graveyard. Student work on the walls is sparse. Instead, weathered and faded posters are distributed around the classroom with vague and pointless phrases like "You can do it" and "We are all readers." The classroom is usually quiet, save for the teacher's voice. You can feel the tension in the room.

A teacher-facilitated classroom has desks in pods where students can easily work together in a collaborative manner. Not only is student work prominently displayed around the classroom, but material for students to use is also present around the room. You can feel the excitement in the room as students work together to solve problems and work together on projects.

Teachers can support collaboration in the classroom by setting up their classroom environment in a way that promotes teamwork and cooperation. Principals can encourage teachers to do this by providing them with classroom furniture to facilitate group work. For example, teachers can arrange desks in small groups or clusters to encourage collaboration and interaction among students. They can also use round tables and other larger workspaces for group work. Designated areas for group work will make the classroom a more interactive space for students.

What Now?

This section is geared for modeling. If we want teachers to change their instructional habits, we need to model these best practices for them. Here's how to get started.

1. Mix up the seating for your faculty meetings. I used to hold mine in the library. I liked to decide where the "front" would be after everyone had sat down. Sometimes the back became the front and everyone who sat in the back had to be more engaged. Another idea is to hold your meetings in a teacher's classroom who is creative with their seating arrangement.

2. Turn faculty meetings into work sessions. No one likes to be talked at for an hour, especially teachers who have been working hard all day. Create a choice board for your teachers or have them work on a passion project to encourage high levels of engagement.

3. Start creating a library of ideas for project-based learning for your school. Bring in pictures, posts, and lesson guides from other schools that can spark the interest of your teachers.

Chapter 11

Classroom Observations (Walkthroughs and Instructional Rounds)

C onducting classroom walkthroughs (CWTs) is not a new concept. Educators have been walking through classrooms, gauging instructional practices for years. Unfortunately, CWTs are often conducted due to mandates from the district office downtown and not from the internal desire to improve educational practices. Administrators often go through the motions of walking through without the school getting the benefits of this researched-based activity.

In addition, teachers are missing out on being a part of this important process. Both novice and veteran teachers alike can benefit from classroom walkthroughs. These walkthroughs should be planned out, purposeful, and conducted routinely through-out the year.

CWTs are like the part in a horror movie when a singular character goes down to the dark basement to see if their friends are all right.

Don't go it alone.

CWTs are not meant to be conducted in isolation. Having an administrator walk through classrooms taking notes is a good start. Having teachers walk through classrooms with administration is even better. This is the shift between classroom walkthroughs and instructional rounds (IRs). In utilizing IRs, the teachers conducting the walkthroughs can debrief after each visit, discussing what strategies the classroom teacher was utilizing, what worked, and what they might do differently in their own classroom.

Instructional rounds are a collaborative professional development strategy that involves teams of educators observing and discussing classroom instruction to improve teaching and learning. Instructional rounds are typically conducted in teams of four to six educators, including teachers, administrators, and instructional coaches.

During instructional rounds, the team of educators visits classrooms to observe instruction and collect data on teaching practices. The team then meets to discuss their observations and analyze the data collected. Instructional rounds are a disciplined way for educators to work together to improve instruction (City, Elmore, Fiarman, & Teitel, 2009).

This process allows educators to identify areas of strength and areas for improvement in instructional practices, as well as to share ideas and strategies for improving teaching and learning. The most important part of the instructional rounds process is the debriefing and conversation that happens after each observation.

Instructional rounds are based on the idea that effective teaching and learning require ongoing professional development and collaboration among educators. By observing and discussing classroom instruction, educators can learn from each other, improve their own teaching practices, and promote a culture of continuous improvement in their schools.

Instructional rounds typically involve several stages, including planning, observation, debriefing, and action planning. Substitute teachers need to be secured in order to ensure that teachers can have their classes covered and be a part of the process. Overall, the process is designed to be nonevaluative and focused on improvement and sharing of best practices rather than on individual teacher performance.

Too often, CWTs are conducted when an administrator has a free moment. Principals try to visit classrooms in between speaking with an angry parent, working with a child sent to the office on a disciplinary issue, and covering a classroom due to a substitute teacher not showing up. They'll visit a classroom here or there, but never get to enough rooms to be able to collect sufficient data to see trends. CWTs need to be a priority. Time must be scheduled each and every day so that every classroom can be visited at least once per week.

I'll repeat that. Every classroom. Every week.

Yes. It is a tall order.

Yes, time will need to be blocked out on your calendar to make this happen.

Yes, I'm serious.

Every classroom. Every week.

To give some context, I conduct these classroom visits in schools with up to 40 classrooms. This number is much more manageable than trying to fit in classroom visits at a comprehensive high school with 100+ classrooms. For large schools, it will be impossible to have one person visit every classroom every week. This is where coordinating with assistant principals will be vital as all administrators will need to divide and conquer to ensure that they meet the end result of visiting every classroom every week.

Regardless of the size of the school, many principals struggle with getting out of the office to visit classrooms. Here is the trick to doing just that.

Empower your office staff.

The office staff must be on board with this priority. I would block the time on my shared calendar and let my office staff know that I would be in classrooms for the next hour. I would also tell them that I was leaving my walkie-talkie in my office.

I know. Crazy, right? Here's the thing, you don't have to take your radio everywhere. I am willing to bet that you have a cell phone and that your office staff has your number. In an emergency, they can text you to come back to the office. I routinely told my office staff that there were three reasons to call me when I was in classrooms:

1. The police are on campus.
2. The school is on fire.
3. Someone is hurt.

Everything else could wait.

Children do get hurt on the playground and need to see the school nurse. At the middle school level, I did frequently interact with police officers for a variety of reasons, some related to things that happened on campus, some because the officers knew that the students would be at school at that time.

When these issues came up while I was visiting classrooms, I always returned to the office. It is important that you not leave your office staff hanging. In doing so, you will lose credibility, and you can't afford to have an office staff that doesn't trust you or your word.

I also informed parents of this practice as well. I would routinely insert a message into my newsletter stating that I am enjoying getting into their children's classrooms frequently and that this was a priority for me and the staff. I apologized up front for the possibility that I would not be available to meet with them if they came to the school unannounced looking for me.

Chances are, the school is not going to burn down if you get out of your office to visit classrooms on a frequent basis. Again, your staff has your cell phone number. Trust me, if it is an emergency, they'll find you.

After a few weeks, enough data will be collected in order to see department, grade level, and school-wide instructional trends. Be sure to visit classrooms at different times of the day. It is fascinating to see how the data can change depending on a morning or afternoon visit.

Collecting data will not be of any service to anyone unless it is shared, analyzed, discussed, and acted upon. I recommend sharing CWT data once a month with staff members. Data can be broken down by grade, department, or individual teacher. Remember to be clinical, not critical, with the analysis. Names of teachers or classrooms should never be used as CWT data analysis should not be used as a "gotcha." You want your staff to embrace and discuss the data, not be defensive.

Use the data to decide where you need to go with professional development. Walkthroughs can shed light on a variety of different instructional elements, including student engagement, groupings, depth of knowledge (DOK) levels, student and teacher actions, as well as classroom environment. Select the biggest area of need and provide ongoing professional development in that area.

Many teachers get stressed out when another educator comes into their room to watch them teach. Even worse is having that educator leave the classroom without providing any sort of feedback. The teacher is left wondering if the visitor liked what they saw or if their instruction is seen as a cause for concern. To avoid this anxiety, leave a Post-it note on the teacher's desk at the end of your CWT. Pick out one positive instructional element and praise them for it. This will put them at ease and open the door for future conversations about CWT data in the future that might not be so pleasant.

What Now?

Conducting classroom observations is a powerful way to change the culture of your school. If you are stepping into a school that does not have a history of frequent observations, here are a few ways to get started on the right foot.

1. Share the purpose of observations with your staff. It must be clearly communicated that observations are to benefit everyone and to highlight all of the wonderful things happening in classrooms on a daily basis. These are not evaluative. Teachers need to hear that.
2. Create an observation schedule in your calendar. Start this at the beginning of the year in order to solidify the routine from the start.

3. Your first observations should be with your middle-ground teachers. Starting with your go-getters might create the notion of favoritism. Starting with your struggling teachers or the ones who need the biggest culture shift might raise too many alarms. Starting with your middle-ground teachers will give you the opportunity to begin in a neutral space and bring these teachers in on the experience.

Chapter 12

Implementing Instructional Technology

When I started my administrative journey, edtech was just getting going. There were a variety of simple digital assessment tools out there, several word processing programs, and a few digital presentation options for students to explore. Students at schools everywhere were starting to learn how to get online and research different topics, email their teachers for help, and dig deeper into making real-world connections to their content.

However, my middle school looked awfully similar to the schools I attended in the late 1980s and early 1990s. We had chalkboards, not whiteboards. There wasn't a computer lab. Teachers had one computer in their classrooms. One. And that computer was for the teacher, not for students.

Amazon sold its first item in 1995.

Google became available to the world in 1998.

Facebook was launched in 2004.

My school had chalkboards and one computer per classroom in 2006. Think about this: My school was located in San Jose, California, a stone's throw away from the heart of Silicon Valley. The world headquarters for Apple, Google, Adobe, and Facebook were all a short drive away.

We also did not have air conditioning, but that is another story. For those of you unfamiliar with the weather in San Jose, it can get above 100 degrees at the beginning and end of the school year.

The first course of action was to create a technology committee, composed of teachers and parents. It was important to hear what they wanted for instructional technology and how it could be used to support student learning. I was excited about this new direction for the school. That was until we sat down for our first meeting.

I can still hear the words. "I don't use technology."

This is what my teachers started with.

As a new principal, I was taken aback a bit, and didn't quite know how to respond. I wasn't expecting to open the meeting in this manner.

And that was just the beginning.

We were still using paper attendance sheets that were brought to the office every period. Newsletters were printed each month and sent home in backpacks. Students completed worksheet after worksheet and routinely handwrote 2- to 3-page papers.

We needed a new path. We needed to prepare our students for their future, not our past. We needed to get comfortable with being uncomfortable.

Many schools make the mistake of putting the cart before the horse. They let the technology drive instruction and purchase computers, programs, and other hardware without a plan to connect them to the content. The reverse needs to happen.

Instruction should always drive technology, not the other way around.

As a committee, we started to redefine our learning outcomes and how we wanted our students to demonstrate mastery of the content using current technology. We came up with three non-negotiables:

1. All students and teachers need to be literate in current technology.
2. All students need to have access to technology on a regular basis at school.
3. All teachers need to integrate technology into instructional plans.

A one-to-one environment at the time was unheard of. Computers were still too expensive to purchase one for every student. Desktop computers were still the most popular option. Cheaper options, such as Chromebooks, were years away.

The school was run on a shoestring budget. We were a Title 1 district, but not a Title 1 school. I ran all school operations on about $30,000 after salaries, benefits, maintenance, board-adopted curriculum, and utilities. Without a ton of money to work with, we got busy applying for grants, and were able to secure some additional funding.

Our first purchase was a mobile laptop cart that could be brought to classrooms or set up in our school's library.

Fun fact: A mobile computer cart was often called a COW. No, not because it weighed a ton. *COW* was an acronym for Computers on Wheels. COW.

Having a COW allowed every student to get on a device. We created a sign-up sheet for teachers to either request the cart or have the laptop set up in the library. We monitored the sign-up sheet and encouraged all teachers to get into a rotation of using the laptops.

At first, it was very slow.

Only a few teachers were signing up for the cart. Most were reluctant to use these new devices. That reluctance came from the fact that teachers didn't know what to do with the technology. Ignorance is bliss. It is easier to do things the way they have always been done. I realized that if teachers were going to change how they looked at instruction, I would have to model that change for them.

At every opportunity I could, I modeled the type of technology usage that I wanted to see in classrooms. I ensured that laptops were out at every staff meeting and that we used them for research, feedback, or data analysis.

Principals need to be able to model the change they want to see in their teachers. Teachers need to see that their principal understands the changes and can be successful in the implementation of new technology. This doesn't mean principals need to become a school-based version of the Apple Bar, but they should be able to troubleshoot, set up, and use the technology available at the school.

This notion was further tested when I brought SMART Boards to the school a year later. Thanks to a library block grant, I was able to purchase a SMART Board for every teacher at the school. Admittedly, this was newer technology at the time, and I wasn't 100% aware of all of the teaching and learning capabilities that came with the implementation of these boards.

I had the boards installed over the summer, complete with a hanging LCD projector from the ceiling. I began my third year as a principal walking into the lion's den. I had transitioned the instruction at the school from solely pencil and paper to using laptops and software to engage and assess students. I compare that first journey to the Wright brothers' first flight at Kitty Hawk; this would be more like landing a spacecraft on the moon.

We started small. Baby steps. Actually, it was more like a crawl. We celebrated every movement forward. We started with just turning it on and hooking up their computers. While many teachers were very reluctant to use this new technology, I had a few who were excited. We began to hold our staff meetings in their rooms, so that these teachers could further model the technology.

I focused on one teacher at a time until I had enough teachers to create a professional learning community around using this new technology. That way, I could then focus my attention on the teachers who were really struggling.

In order to inspire them, we celebrated every use of the technology, every win, and even the losses, as it was important to acknowledge the fact that teachers were trying. It was important also to acknowledge the difference between digital immigrants and digital natives. A digital immigrant is someone who grew up without using many of our current technologies. Digital natives are people who only know of a world with smartphones, Wi-Fi, social media, and digital messaging.

Using new technology is one thing. Using it to enhance instruction is another.

Thousands of dollars were spent on computers, SMART Boards, wiring, Wi-Fi, and programs. Now, it was time to ensure that these tools would be used to take our instructional programs to the next level. My classroom walkthroughs became more detailed, more targeted. I wanted to see this new technology in action. Teachers were a bit hesitant about this approach; they questioned if I expected to see them and their students using the new devices every time I walked in the room.

This is a common question and there is only one answer. No.

Technology should never be used in the classroom just to satisfy a mandate or expectation. It should be used to inform instructional practices and to enhance the learning experience for students. As I conducted my walkthroughs, hitting every classroom once per week, I was able to see trends, simple usage rates, as well as use cases. I highlighted these applications of the technology at staff meetings, in newsletters, and at parent meetings. I talked them up at district meetings and with other principals.

Soon, we became the school to visit to see instructional technology use at its best. Three years prior, we were providing an education experience to our students that was similar to the one I got in the 1980s. Now, we were on the cutting edge, forward thinking, and providing our students with learning experiences needed to prepare them for their future, not our past.

A good school technology plan should consider various elements to effectively integrate technology into the learning environment. It should begin with clearly defining the vision and goals of the school regarding technology integration. This should align with the overall school mission and include objectives related to improving student learning outcomes, enhancing teaching practices, fostering digital literacy, and promoting equitable access to technology resources.

It is vital that the committee evaluate and plan for the necessary technological infrastructure, including reliable internet connectivity, network infrastructure, hardware devices, and software applications. Consider the availability of appropriate resources such as computers, tablets, interactive whiteboards, multimedia equipment, and educational software to support teaching and learning.

Ongoing professional development opportunities for teachers and staff to build their technology skills, pedagogical knowledge, and instructional strategies are essential. School leaders need to offer workshops, training sessions, or online courses to enhance their teachers' and staff members' understanding of effective technology integration and to empower them to utilize technology tools effectively in the classroom.

Committee members should identify areas where technology can enhance and transform learning experiences, and ensure alignment with educational standards. Develop guidelines and resources to support teachers in designing technology-rich, engaging, and meaningful lessons and assessments. The plan should also promote responsible digital citizenship and educate students about appropriate online behavior, internet safety, information literacy, and digital rights and responsibilities. Establish policies and procedures to ensure the privacy, security, and ethical use of technology within the school community.

It is vital that there be mechanisms in place to evaluate the impact and effectiveness of technology integration. Define metrics and indicators to measure the outcomes of technology initiatives, such as improvements in student achievement, engagement, and digital literacy. Use formative and summative assessment strategies to monitor progress and make informed decisions for future planning.

Ensuring a comprehensive and responsible technology budget is an essential operation of a technology committee. Members need to develop a budget plan that accounts for the procurement, maintenance, and upgrades of technology resources. Consider long-term sustainability and funding sources for technology initiatives. Seek partnerships and grants to supplement the budget and ensure ongoing support for technology integration.

Once a plan has been created, school leaders can provide support to foster collaboration and communication among all stakeholders, including teachers, students, parents, administrators, and the broader community, by encouraging open dialogue and feedback, and ensuring that technology initiatives align with the needs and expectations of all stakeholders. Furthermore, the plan should address the digital divide by ensuring equitable access to technology resources for all students, regardless of socioeconomic background or ability. Explore strategies such as device lending programs, community partnerships, or technology grants to bridge the gap and provide equal opportunities for all learners.

Finally, principals need to emphasize a culture of continuous improvement and flexibility. Regularly review and revise the technology plan based on changing needs, emerging trends, and feedback from stakeholders. School leaders should always encourage innovation and exploration of new technologies that can enhance teaching and learning experiences.

What Now?

Understanding instructional technology is no longer something that we'd all like to do, but something that we must do. It can be difficult to make decisions on what to purchase, when to purchase it, how to install it, and how to train staff to use it. If you are feeling like you are headed down the information superhighway with blinders on, here are some ways to get started.

1. Take stock of what your school has already purchased. Get a sense of how old the technology is, what maintenance costs look like, and how viable the technology will be over the next five years. How soon might it become obsolete?
2. Now that you know what you have, understand how it is being used and who is using it. Just because instructional technology tools exist on campus doesn't mean that they are being used. Remember, schools are full of closets of unused and, in some situations, not-yet-unwrapped technology.
3. Are these tools being used with fidelity? In other words, is your school getting their money's worth out of these tools or was money wasted? Do teachers need more training? Have new teachers received any training? Never assume that younger teachers will know how to use these tools just because of their age.

Chapter 13
Assessment for Learning

ssessment has become a "four-letter word" in education. Everywhere you turn, assessments are being dragged through the mud. Educators have been arguing for years that we assess too much, too frequently, and with too much high-stakes pressure.

They are not wrong.

However, assessments can be quite useful, informative, and purposeful when utilized properly. We need to shift our perspective on assessments and begin to assess for learning, and not give assessments of learning. Assessments need to inform instructional next steps as well as give educators a chance to reflect on what is working and what needs to change. Unfortunately, assessments are often used to put a grade on a report card or as a district compliance measure, and once given, the results are never analyzed. Even worse, sometimes assessment results are not available for months, giving educators no time to digest the data and create action plans for their students in order to make a difference.

We need to create smaller, more frequent assessments to assess for learning. Assessments do not have to be summative as they do not allow time for the teacher to go back and reteach what their students missed. Creating smaller, more frequent assessments that serve as "checking for understanding" measures will help a teacher guide their instruction to meet students' current needs.

Teachers will also be able to slow down or approach the content from another direction if need be, based on the data. An instructional pivot can happen in the moment, not weeks or months out.

Assessment for learning is like a baseball coach helping a player during practice. The coach can guide the player on body positioning, bat speed, hand placement, and hand-eye coordination. Adjustments can be made in the moment. Assessment of learning is what happens in the game. While players can make changes after a game, it is in practice sessions where the real work takes place and progress is made.

The National Foundation for Educational Research in the UK recognizes that assessment for learning should be embedded in day-to-day classroom practice as a means of continuously assessing knowledge, informing teaching, and providing feedback to improve pupil learning. Strategies include effective questioning techniques, quality feedback, self-assessment and peer assessment, and using summative tests for formative purposes. (See Figure 13.1.)

Use assessment results need to guide instruction. Assessment results should be used to create leveled groups within a classroom for the purpose of targeting student needs. Assessments need to be created so that the data can be broken down by standard, allowing the teacher to design targeted instruction. In addition, teachers can create follow-up instruction for students who need remediation as well as for students who need accelerated or expanded learning opportunities.

Assessments don't have to be a worksheet. Nothing sparks fear or boredom in a student more than a traditional paper-and-pencil test. Switch it up. Teachers should try introducing Project-based Learning, oral reports, multimedia presentations, or demonstrations that are directly related to real-world scenarios.

I was a terrible test taker. Answering dozens of multiple-choice questions made me anxious before, during, and after the assessment. Many students who would have performed poorly on traditional tests will flourish on more creative and engaging types of assessments. I know I would have performed better.

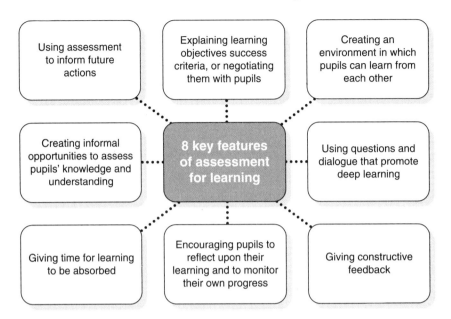

Figure 13.1   8 Key Features of Assessment for Learning
SOURCE: National Foundation for Educational Research.

Furthermore, real-world assessments are more in line with the types of tasks our students will need to perform as adults. Think about it, how often in your career do you sit down and bubble in a test or write short-answer responses to questions? How often in anyone's career?

Assessment question types should be varied and diverse. Creating an assessment that has 30 multiple choice questions might be easy to score, but does it really measure a student's depth of knowledge? Questions should be varied to include open-ended responses, inquiries, fact-finding, and defending. Teachers should get away from having students simply regurgitate answers. This does not lead to long-term knowledge retention. Answers will quickly be forgotten after the test has been completed. Assessment questions should access higher-level Bloom's Taxonomy and Webb's Depth of Knowledge levels 3 and 4 and ask students to assess, revise, critique, construct, prove, and apply the knowledge they have learned.

This leads to long-term knowledge retention as students are applying content to the real world.

Assessment results should be used to create leveled groups within a classroom for the purpose or targeting student needs. Useful assessments can be broken down by standard or domain, allowing the teacher to design targeted instruction.

Results should not be a secret. Ensure that scores are getting back to students and parents so that they are aware of progress made and what needs to happen next. In getting back to the purpose of assessing for learning, the results need to be actionable. It is impossible to act upon assessment results if no one knows what they are.

The American education system is ranked by summative assessment results. This is a reality that all educators need to face. While we can all acknowledge that it is unfair to judge the achievement of a student and the work of teachers based on a few days of tests, it is the world we live in. We will not do our students and communities any good by bucking the system and ignoring this reality.

My students always performed well on state assessments, because of our attention to assessment for learning. We could support our students on particular standards based on our formative assessment results.

The point is to play the game, but be smart about it. Some school leaders skew scores by having only certain students take certain classes. If students are placed in classes based on academic strengths and areas of growth, teachers will be able to attend to their specific needs and prepare them not just for a summative assessment, but for a variety of formative assessments for learning along the way.

What Now?

This is where getting into classrooms is vital. This is also where PLCs are useful. Teachers need to discuss formative assessment regularly to truly understand where their students are on the learning continuum. Principals usually get to review benchmark data, but not when we are assessing for learning. Here is how to get started:

1. Visit PLCs. Principals should not take over PLCs, but should drop in to ensure that the right work is being done. The right work is centered around looking at data.
2. Ask all teachers of a grade level or subject how their students performed on the latest formative assessment. These informal discussions can be very eye-opening and tell you whether or not these assessments are even happening.
3. Ask students how they are performing in a particular class. If they can tell you, it usually means that they are being frequently assessed for learning. If they can't tell you how they are doing, that gives you another important piece of information.

Tales from the Principal's Desk

As I stated earlier, I was worried about my ability to provide rich, actionable feedback to teachers when it came to instructional practices. Remember, I did not consider myself a master teacher; however, I did know what good instruction looked like.

Good instruction was:

- Teacher-facilitated
- Tied to real-world situations
- Collaborative
- Active
- Engaging
- Multimodal
- Differentiated

The main thing I looked for was student engagement. Were students actively involved in the learning process? Were they in the driver's seat, or just passengers on their academic journey? I was not interested in the sit-and-get model of instruction where students sat in "cemetery" seating.

I'll explain cemetery seating here. Cemetery seating refers to students sitting in parallel rows and columns that do not facilitate any collaborative learning, partner or group work, or any discussion of any kind except for the teacher talking at students.

I wanted a way to track student engagement. The only way to do that was to be in classrooms as much as possible. That is when I developed my plan.

I dedicated an entire week to being in classrooms. While I did not specifically tell teachers what I was doing, as I did not want any dog-and-pony shows, I did tell them that I would be in classrooms more often and for longer periods of time than usual. My goal was to track the amount of minutes per class period that students were actively engaged in the learning process.

Armed with a clipboard and a timer, I got to work.

It was a long week. I made it to every classroom, some twice. I stayed for an entire class period of 52 minutes and tracked engagement. At the end of the week, I calculated my results and got the average number of minutes per class period that students were actively engaged in the learning process.

I was shocked at the results.

11 minutes.

That's 11 minutes out of a 52-minute period.

That's barely 20% of the class period. The other 41 minutes were used, on average, for taking attendance, transitions, homework collection, classroom management issues, seat work, silent reading, and just straight-up downtime.

Remember, it's not how many minutes you have to work with, it's what you do with them. Based on the data I collected, we could have shortened the school day to just an hour and a half and students would've gotten that same amount of time being actively engaged in their classrooms. The results of this study were troubling, but not the only problem I was going to deal with.

I had to share the data with the staff.

I knew what I would be up against. I prepared myself for the comments to come.

"This is just your opinion."

"You just saw one class period. The next class was about to work much more."

"You should've brought a teacher with you."

I did not want to get into a battle with my teachers in regard to the data, but I also needed them to understand that we couldn't go on like this. We needed to change things up. Before I presented the data to my teachers, I did have a few teacher volunteers conduct a few more observations with me. I chose a veteran teacher (who was not a fan of me), a newer teacher, and a mid-career teacher who often served as a go-between from the staff to administration. I set up the parameters of the observations and ensured that they agreed on what to look for.

They came up with the same times.

I had my leverage. This was my moment.

I created a bunch of color graphs and charts highlighting the data for each grade level, department, and cluster. I did not use any identifying titles or names. While I knew what data belonged to sixth grade, the teachers did not. They just knew that the data represented a grade level at the school.

There was shock, anger, disbelief, tears, resentment, and frustration. Obviously, it was all directed at me. That is, until I shared that the teachers who also conducted observations also came up with the same results.

You could hear a pin drop in the library.

As I talked through the data, I remained clinical, not critical. I did not point fingers or come down on any grade level, department, or individual teacher. I'll be honest here: It didn't help much. There was no magical epiphany. Rather than drag out the uncomfortable vibe any longer, I ended the meeting and asked everyone to reflect upon the data and what we discussed.

The next few days were rough.

On one side, I got the cold shoulder, the side-eye, the judging glare, and the silent treatment. On the other side, I got yelled at, talked about in the staff room and hallways, and sent less than encouraging emails.

I decided to up the ante. I decided to run the next staff meeting using the data totals from the observations. I planned on only making 11% of the meeting active. The rest would be quiet seat work or wasted time.

Now, I feel like I should tell everyone reading this book that I don't necessarily endorse this plan or recommend that you try it at your school. However, I wasn't going to just sit by and allow our students to miss out.

Our staff meetings were on Tuesdays. To say I was nervous would be an understatement. I spent the afternoon before our meeting in my office preparing for the worst, but also getting ready to prove a point. I made my way to the library during the last period of the day. I placed a packet on the tables in front of each chair, one for every teacher. As teachers began to shuffle in for the meeting, I did not greet them, only told them to find a seat and to wait for instructions.

I began our staff meeting exactly on time. A few teachers were late coming in and I asked them to find a seat quickly and quietly. Then, I gave them their instructions.

In front of them was a section of our school's safety plan. Eighteen pages, to be exact. I told them to read this section and to mark any changes that were needed in the margins. I asked them to complete this task silently. You could cut the tension with a knife.

Some teachers started to work their way through the document. Others flat out refused and just sat there. There was a lot of confusion in the room.

I let this go on for 15 minutes. I worried that if it went on any longer, teachers were going to storm out and that I would end up paying a bigger price than I had bargained for. I told everyone to put their pens down and explained what was happening. Some teachers were angry, but others were reflective and acknowledged that they were guilty of using similar methods in their classroom. Conversations started happening. Anger turned to realization. Reluctance turned into acceptance.

The next 45 minutes were more like group therapy than a staff meeting. I let the conversation go where it needed to, only bringing it back in when it was time to wrap it up for the day. As we ended our meeting and teachers got up to leave for the day, one of the more veteran teachers headed right for me. This teacher in particular had been giving me a hard time for the past two years. I prepared myself for the worst, but it never came.

"We needed that."

I was floored. I could not believe that she understood the point I was trying to make. I knew that if she was on my side, I could move the other reluctant teachers. From that day on, she and I had an understanding. We didn't always get along, but there was a new mutual respect between us. I also now had an ally who was well respected among the teachers who did not like the changes that were happening at the school.

And that meant everyone.

Questions to Ask Yourself

- Are our instructional practices aligned with our assessment strategies and goals? Reflect on the alignment between the instructional practices employed in the classroom and the assessment strategies used to measure student learning. Consider whether the methods and tools used for instruction align with the intended learning outcomes and the assessments used to evaluate student progress.
- How well are we differentiating instruction and assessment to meet the needs of all students? Note how effectively instruction and assessment practices cater to the diverse needs and abilities of students. Consider whether teachers are employing differentiated instructional strategies that accommodate various learning styles, abilities, and interests. Assess whether assessment practices are differentiated to provide opportunities for all students to demonstrate their knowledge and skills in ways that are accessible and meaningful to them.
- How are we using assessment data to inform instruction and improve student learning? Think about how assessment data is

collected, analyzed, and utilized to inform instructional decisions. Consider whether teachers have the necessary support and resources to effectively analyze assessment data and identify areas of student strengths and areas in need of improvement. Assess whether there are systems in place to provide timely and actionable feedback to students and to adjust instructional strategies based on assessment results. Reflect on how well assessment data is used to drive instructional improvement and student growth.

Pillar III

Community

Chapter 14

We're Not
in Kansas Anymore

I remember my initial visit to my school when I became an administrator for the first time. I flew from Southern California to Northern California in the morning to have a final interview with district leaders. In truth, there were two schools that had assistant principal openings. I would be the first hire. I asked if I could go visit each school, just to get an idea of what they looked like, even if it was only from the outside. I was told I could visit and to let them know if I had a preference.

At that time, I was a teacher in the beach community of Carlsbad, a beach town about 35 miles north of downtown San Diego. Carlsbad is a wealthy community. Students were dropped off in cars three times more expensive than mine. I drove a Jetta at the time. The parents of my students were doctors, lawyers, sales executives, scientists, and entrepreneurs. My new district was located in east San Jose. While the district was only about 15 minutes from downtown San Jose, the community had no resemblance to the Silicon Valley that is represented in movies and on social media. The schools did not look like they did, either.

On my drive to the district office from the airport, I noticed something very different from where I currently was teaching and living. Most of the business signs were in Spanish.

It was summer break, so there weren't any students at either school. The campuses were quiet except for the sound of maintenance work. The schools were fenced in, so I could only look in from the outside. The grass was browned out, there was still trash in the common areas. Maintenance workers were trying to paint over graffiti.

I knew immediately which school I wanted: the one tucked into the foothills in a quiet community. I could see the quad area from the parking lot and immediately began to see the possibilities. I gave the district my request and started to drive back to the airport.

Two months later, my wife and I moved to the Bay Area and I began my administrative career.

At first, I was intimidated by the community. Signs were in Spanish, people around town spoke Spanish, and often looked at me like I was lost. I knew that in order to be successful, I needed to be comfortable in the community and that my community needed to be comfortable with me. I knew my less than stellar Spanish skills weren't going to get me far. I had to find another way.

What Now?

I don't recommend the path I took. I was unfamiliar with the community before I accepted the position. If the opportunity had presented itself differently, here is what I would have done:

1. Research the community. I'll discuss this further in the next chapter.
2. Drive around. Note the local stores, businesses, parks, and resources. Begin to understand what is located within the community.
3. Keep an open mind. Many of my first impressions were at the surface level. That was a mistake. A community goes much deeper than what you can see from the window of a car.

Chapter 15
School and Community Research

There is a substantial body of research suggesting that building strong relationships between schools and communities is critical for the success of both. Schools that create healthy bonds enjoying strong relationships with their neighborhoods tend to have better academic performance. These schools have higher reading and math scores, higher graduation rates, and lower drop-out rates as compared with schools that lack support among parents, businesses, and government.

When schools work to build relationships with their communities, parents are more likely to participate in their child's education. This involvement can take many forms, including volunteering in the classroom or elsewhere in the school, attending school events, and participating in parent-teacher conferences. This higher level of participation can lead to increased academic performance, better attendance, and a more positive school culture for students and staff alike.

When parents are active in their children's education, they can provide additional assistance and resources, such as tutoring, homework help, and access to educational materials. This additional guidance can help children to better understand and retain what they are learning in school.

Healthy parental involvement can help to foster robust bonds between parents, children, and teachers. When parents are active in their children's education, they are better able to communicate with teachers and stay informed about their child's progress in school. This can help to identify areas where children may be struggling and can lead to early intervention to address these issues. In addition, when parents have a strong relationship with their child's teacher, they are better able to advocate for their child's needs and can work together with the teacher to create a personalized plan for academic success.

Furthermore, parental involvement can help to build a sense of community within the school. When parents are involved in school activities and events, they become part of the school community and can help to create a healthy and supportive environment for all students. This sense of camaraderie can encourage a culture of academic integrity leading to improved learning outcomes.

When schools work to build relationships with their communities, it can help to create a more positive and supportive school climate. Local businesses and agencies can provide extracurricular activities, such as after-school programs, and mental health programs, which can help to enhance the overall well-being of students and staff. Community members can also help to provide intern programs for students interested in learning a craft, trade, or business. Furthermore, having that program offering come from the surrounding area of the school community adds a level of local pride and improvement from within.

Communities can provide additional program possibilities to schools. This can include financial assets, such as donations and grants, which can be used to fund important initiatives, such as technology upgrades, specialty teachers, building renovations, after-school programs, and educational programs. In addition, communities can provide in-kind resources, such as volunteer time and expertise, which can be used to support a range of initiatives, such as mentoring programs, after-school programs, and mental health services. By partnering with community organizations, schools can provide students with access to extracurricular activities, such as sports teams, music programs, and art classes.

Local organizations can provide important supports, such as school resource officers and mental health professionals, to ensure that students have a safe and healthy environment in which to learn. Community members can also serve as role models for students, and can help to promote a culture of respect, tolerance, and inclusion.

What Now?

The reach of a school is not limited to the walls or fences that surround the perimeter, but can be felt throughout an entire community. Principals who are new to their school's community need to ask the following questions:

1. What does parental involvement look like at the school? If it is high, continue to improve on what is working by increasing inclusion. If it is low, create a committee of mostly parents and a few teachers to get a sense of what would help to jump-start parental involvement. Be careful not to repeat what has not worked in the past.
2. What businesses in the community have partnered with the school to provide programs for students? Nurture these relationships and highlight the businesses that are participating. Set a goal of bringing in 1–2 new partnerships a year.
3. Does the school collaborate with any mental health partners? If not, find out what opportunities are in the local neighborhood and create a partnership with them to help support students and their families outside of the school day.

Chapter 16
Using Social Media in Schools

Social media has transformed communication. Pictures, videos, and comments can be easily posted and sent to followers instantly from around the corner or from the other side of the world. For administrators and teachers, social media gives them another opportunity to share activities, programs, and student learning with the surrounding community.

However, schools continue to lag behind the rest of industry in this area, because of safety concerns, general trepidation, or lack of knowledge. It is important that we educators write our own story before someone else writes it for us.

Teachers spend their entire day working with students. They engage them in thoughtful, exciting, and innovative projects, conversations, and ideas. As a parent, I would love to see and hear more of these interactions. Working parents who do not have the flexibility to volunteer on a regular basis in their child's classroom, however, miss out on experiencing day-to-day interactions. Posting images on social media will give them a window into that world from anywhere.

Principals can share important updates, announcements, and news in real time to parents and community members via social media. They can also respond to questions, concerns, and feedback from stakeholders, improving transparency and fostering a stronger sense of community. It is no longer needed for a parent to make an appointment to see the principal in their office in order to get an answer to a question.

A word of caution here.

It is important to remember that social media is public. Content and conversations need to be carefully crafted. Unlike public attitudes toward musicians and celebrities, no one wants to see a school leader get into a fight with a parent on Twitter. Keep posts light, fun, and broad.

Examples of good posts:
  Pictures of the playground
  Showcases of student projects
  Awards
  Early out and vacation reminders
  Calendar events

Examples of posts you should avoid:
  Students in classrooms where they are off task
  Pictures with litter or graffiti
  Using names or student faces without permission
  Anything remotely controversial

Over the years, I have discovered a tremendous amount of professional development outlets via Twitter, Instagram, Facebook, and TikTok. I regularly participate in different educational chats and discussions with educators from around the country and the world. I follow hashtags relevant to my areas of interest.

Here are some popular hashtags to check out:
General education: #edchat, #blendlearning, #whatisschool, #edreform #k12 #schools #education #teachers
School administration: #principals #edadmin #edleaders #edleadership #schoolprincipal
Education technology: #edtech #edutech, #21stedchat, #blendlearning

Give yourself a half hour to go exploring. Trust me, you'll be hooked.

Having students use social media can strike fear into even the most progressive educator; however, we all know that many students are already on social media. It is vital that we teach them to be responsible while they are online and with what they post. We need to help students develop their voice, while at the same time ensuring they do not leave a digital footprint that will haunt them for years to come.

Social media can be a powerful tool for students to enhance their learning experience, communicate with their peers and teachers, and showcase their work. It should also not be limited to just the popular social media platforms. Tools such as Trello, Slack, Google Chat, and Jamboard can also be considered social media. Students can use these alternative social media platforms like Google Drive, Dropbox, or Trello to collaborate on projects and share resources with their peers. These social media tools can facilitate group discussions, brainstorming, and idea-sharing.

According to Georgetown University,

> From elementary school up until university graduation, social media has the role to empower parents, students, and teachers to use new ways of sharing information and build a community. Statistics show that 96% of the students that have internet access are using at least one social network [http://www.bestmastersineducation.com/social-media/]. What's even more extraordinary is that, even though some of the students use the social networks for entertaining and other purposes, there are a lot of them that actually use it to promote a lot of positive and useful activities. From finding a summer internship, promoting a success story about how to win the student-loan battle or collaborate on international projects, everything is made possible. (Wade, 2019)

Teachers should be encouraged to use social media platforms like Twitter, Facebook, or Reddit to create online discussion forums where students can engage in peer-to-peer learning, ask questions, and share their opinions on different topics. This will provide students with a fun way to connect with others using a method they are comfortable with.

Social media can be used as a research tool, allowing students to access a wide range of online resources, such as online databases, news articles, and academic journals. Students can also create digital portfolios showcasing their work and accomplishments. This can include photos, videos, artwork, and writing samples that can be shared with teachers, peers, and future potential employers.

Social media can create online communication between students, teachers, and administrators, allowing for more personalized and responsive feedback. This can include the usual social media platforms where students can tag their teachers in posts, or collaboration platforms like Slack or Microsoft Teams.

Self-directed learning can be facilitated with different social media platforms, allowing students to explore new interests and topics outside the classroom. For example, students can use YouTube channels or education blogs to learn about new subjects, follow experts in their field of interest, and engage in discussions with like-minded individuals.

I have been interested in the notion of school branding for some time now. With parents now having more options in their child's education, I believe that schools need to do a better job in "selling" the mission and vision of the school to the public. Social media should be used as a tool for branding and reputation management. By sharing positive news and updates, such as celebrations of student learning, school leaders can create a positive image for their school community. Showcasing the school's strengths and achievements in this way can help to counter negative perceptions or rumors that may circulate about the school.

It is important for schools to share the day-to-day happenings on campus to parents. Sharing pictures, videos, and comments helps bridge the knowledge gap for parents. As parents become informed, they will be more inclined to step forward to actively volunteer and become active on vital school committees such as School Site Council, PTA, and ELAC.

While I wholeheartedly believe in the use of social media by schools, and that it is a valuable way for schools to communicate with their community, it is important to recognize there are some potential drawbacks if the use of these platforms is not thought out ahead of time.

Social media is a public platform, and schools must be mindful of student privacy concerns. Posting photos, videos, or other content that identifies students could violate their privacy rights, and could also expose them to potential risks, such as cyberbullying or online predators. There can be an information overload for parents and staff. With so much content available, it can be difficult to sift through and prioritize the most important information, which can lead to important messages being missed. Managing social media accounts can be time-consuming and resource intensive. Schools may need to dedicate staff time and resources to create content, manage accounts, and respond to comments or messages.

Social media can be a platform for cyberbullying and trolling, which can have a negative impact on students and the school community. Schools must be proactive in monitoring and addressing negative behavior on social media to ensure that all students feel safe and respected.

Bullying on social media can be a serious problem that can negatively affect students' mental health and well-being. School leaders need to educate students and parents about responsible social media use, including the negative effects of cyberbullying. They can provide resources and guidance on how to identify and report this type of negative conduct. A clear social media policy can set expectations for students, staff, and parents on what is and isn't acceptable comportment on social media. This policy can outline the consequences for those who engage in this unwanted behavior. Administrators can monitor social media activity and encourage students, staff, and parents to report any bullying they observe. Many states have free online tools where anyone can report online bullying to the school anonymously. In cases where this behavior on social media may be criminal, school administrators can work with law enforcement to investigate and address the behavior. Victims of bullying on social media may need support and resources to help them cope with the effects of the misconduct. Schools can provide counseling services, mental health resources, and other support to victims and their families.

Accounts used by schools can be managed by various stakeholders in the school community, including teachers, administrators, and students. This can lead to inconsistent messaging and potentially conflicting information being shared, which can be confusing for parents and students.

Keeping a consistent social media message can be important for schools to establish a clear brand identity; communicate effectively with students, staff, and parents; and build a positive reputation. Principals should create a social media committee so that a dedicated team is in charge of all the accounts.

First, schools should create social media guidelines that clarify the voice and tone of their messaging, the types of content they will share, and how they will respond to comments and feedback. These guidelines should be distributed to all staff members responsible for posting on social media. Second, schools should designate specific staff members to manage and post content on social media. This can help ensure that messaging is consistent and on-brand. Third, a social media content calendar can help schools plan out their social media messaging in advance, ensuring that they are posting regular and consistent content.

Most schools do not have the luxury of having a marketing coordinator on staff. Therefore, school personnel will need to work closely together to establish a clear brand identity that is consistent across all communication channels, including social media. This includes using the same logos, colors, and fonts across all platforms.

Principals need to provide training to staff members responsible for social media management to ensure they understand the guidelines and how to maintain consistency in messaging.

Lastly, schools should regularly monitor their social media engagement and adjust their messaging as necessary. This can include analyzing the types of posts that receive the most engagement and adjusting the content calendar accordingly.

What Now?

Social media is not something that educators should shy away from. It should not only be embraced, but used in a savvy, purposeful way. Here is how to get started:

1. If it doesn't exist, create a social media account for your school on Facebook, Twitter, and Instagram. Publicize these accounts with your school community and encourage everyone to follow them.
2. Use parents and students as photographers. You can't be everywhere. Encourage your community to send you pictures of sporting events, concerts, class projects, meetings, celebrations, and more in order to create a robust calendar of content.
3. Ensure that you have photography waivers on file for every child on campus. If you have some families that do not want their child's photo shared, make sure that you know who they are so that you don't mistakenly post a picture of them. This could create a potential backlash against using social media in the school.

Chapter 17
Know Your Neighborhood

W hen I was a teacher, I had the opportunity to live in the same neighborhood where my school was located. I enjoyed the feeling of being a celebrity as I ran into my students and their parents around town. I shopped in their businesses and ate at their restaurants. I'm not ashamed to admit that I was granted some free upgrades here or there over the years.

I do remember going to the local movie theater one night to watch the first *Lord of the Rings* movie. For those of you who might be too young to have seen it, the movie clocks in at just under three hours. Remember, back then we did not have stadium seating or the ability to select our seats ahead of time. You got what you got.

I bought two tickets at the box office for my wife and me and headed inside to get some popcorn before finding seats. As we entered the theater, we scanned the premises for two seats together that weren't too close to the screen or too far in the back or the sides. Then, like magic, I saw two seats in the middle. As I made my way through the aisle to claim two of the best seats in the house, my elation turned to horror as I heard, "Hi, Mr. Franklin!"

There, in the seat next to the two empty seats was one of my sixth-grade students. And not just any student.

A drummer.

We will call him Kyle.

I sat down next to him, introduced him to my wife, and then pretended like this wasn't weird at all. Luckily for me, the previews started a few minutes later. For the next three hours, I sat next to Kyle, ate my popcorn, and watched the movie.

We didn't talk at all during the movie or after it ended other than my asking him if he enjoyed it. On Monday, he was telling all of his friends about our movie experience. He was quite pleased with himself. After that, our *Lord of the Rings* experiences bonded us in a special way as he got to see me as a regular person outside of school and I got to see him as just a 12-year-old kid in the neighborhood. We had shared an experience that, 20+ years later, I am still thinking about, as it is these memories that stay with both the educator and the student – not the grade that was earned on a midterm exam. It wouldn't have been possible if I hadn't gone to that movie theater located down the street from the school.

It is important to get to know the school's neighborhood.

When I became a principal, I found myself in a very different school neighborhood. Gone were the upscale restaurants and boutique shops. In their place were street vendors, taquerias, bars, and check-cashing stores. The roads were in disrepair, there was graffiti on the walls of stores, and some of the storefronts themselves had crumbling facades.

I felt way out of my comfort zone.

As I stated before, I only spoke a little Spanish and I was worried about my ability to communicate with community members. However, I did have one thing going for me. Growing up in Southern California, I did know good Mexican food when I saw it. I found what could only be described as a hole-in-the-wall taqueria. Now, I am not exaggerating when I say they had the best carne asada burritos I have ever had. One day, the woman behind the counter asked me, half in English and half in Spanish, if I was the principal at the school down the road.

It turns out that she was the aunt of one of my students.

After that, each time I went in to pick up lunch, I got a little something extra in my to-go bag.

I began stopping at the local grocery store on my way home, rather than the store in my own neighborhood, in order to support local businesses. I went to watch my students play soccer at local parks and rec centers.

Although I didn't live in the community, I became a part of the community. Principal Franklin was now a celebrity in a new neighborhood.

Principals play a crucial role in building relationships with the community and fostering a positive school culture. One of the best ways for principals to get to know the community is to attend local events, such as festivals, community fairs, club sports, and town hall meetings. This allows them to meet community members in a more informal setting and learn about their interests and concerns.

Visiting local businesses and introducing themselves to owners can be a great way for principals to learn more about the community's economic landscape and build partnerships with local businesses. Additionally, volunteering in the community, such as at a local food bank or charity event, allows principals to show their commitment to the community and get to know residents outside of the school setting.

Principals can connect with community leaders, such as city council members or religious leaders, to learn about local issues and collaborate on initiatives that benefit the community. Social media can be a powerful tool for principals to connect with the community and share updates about the school. Principals can create social media accounts for the school and engage with community members online.

What Now?

Most new principals work in schools that are not close to home. These new communities will be unfamiliar and therefore can create anxiety for new administrators. If you find yourself in this situation, here are a few things to do right from the start:

1. Stop at the local grocery store on the way home. You might not recognize the parents of your students, but they will recognize you. They will also appreciate you for shopping in their neighborhood.

2. Make a dinner reservation at a local restaurant. If the restaurants in the area don't take reservations, just walk in and wait. You never know who will also be eating there or working as a cook, server, or front of house.

3. If you don't know where to start, go on a Starbucks run. If you can, bring your laptop or a book and hang out for a while. You never know who might just drop by.

Chapter 18

Connecting with the Community

G reat schools have strong communication protocols with parents. The research is quite clear that children of all ages benefit when educators and parents are in constant communication with one another. Sadly, many parents often feel out of touch with their child's school, not knowing about upcoming events or activities. I have felt this way as a parent myself. Schools need to do better. School leaders should have several tools in our communication tool belt.

I love social media. I have found it to be one of the best ways to show parents what is happening at the school throughout the day. I routinely took pictures of great teaching, learning, and special events, and tweeted them out several times per day. It only takes a few seconds to snap a picture, write a caption, and post it. Research suggests that almost half of all students have a smartphone by age 11. That percentage goes to almost 84% by age 17. Additionally, 95% of all adults with school-aged children have a smartphone.

Creating a school social media account could reach the vast majority of your parents and community members. It will also help principals get out of the office and visit classrooms.

It is vital that school leaders and teachers create this online narrative for their school. Otherwise, someone else will write it for them. Sending out positive messages about teachers and students helps to create a positive culture that will spread beyond the school's boundary and into the community as a whole.

I love coffee. I drink several cups a day. I also like donuts.

The idea is simple: Coffee with the Principal.

Parents are tired. Give them coffee and a relaxed, friendly atmosphere and they will come back again and again. Don't make the mistake of creating a jam-packed agenda filled with important school business.

In fact, don't have an agenda at all.

Keep it light and just have a conversation, pour some coffee, and serve some donuts. I was able to get both the coffee and the donuts donated each time from local shops.

If you are struggling to get more dads involved at the school, try a Donuts for Dads morning. Need to know what a dad's favorite donut flavor is?

Two donuts.

There are other versions as well that will bring in other families and community members:

- Tea with Tias ("aunts" in Spanish)
- Mornings with Moms
- Good Mornings with Grandparents
- Good Mornings with Guardians

There don't have to be strategic outcomes, lofty goal-setting conversations, or inspirational messaging happening at these meetings. Just getting parents involved in coming down to the school is a big enough win.

There are also a variety of opportunities to involve community partners such as neighborhood businesses, colleges, and nonprofit agencies in the school. These community partners can help with fundraising, school awareness, student internships, career support, and educational pipelines. Furthermore, many of these opportunities can be found right in front of you.

The first place I would start would be a local library. Have you ever heard of a library turning down a partnership with a school? Me neither. Consider having a library card drive or even hold an afternoon professional development session for your teachers at the library. A change of scenery is most always welcomed. Plus, most libraries don't charge schools for the use of their meeting rooms.

One of the most important partnerships that a school can make is with a college or university. There are many different reasons for this that involve both students and teachers. For students, it is important that they begin to develop an understanding of life after high school from a young age. Many of the students we work with will be first-generation college students and their parents will not have the personal background to navigate the complex world of higher education. By exposing students to college counselors, campus tours, student activities, and different areas of study, they will begin to understand the options that are available to them.

Colleges and universities are also great resources for curating guest speakers and experts from the field. For example, learning about ancient civilizations is sure to be interesting to many students. Consider the increase in engagement and excitement when a professor who has participated on archaeological digs comes in to speak to students, bringing artifacts and items from their explorations. Professors at city and regional colleges can also bring in a local flair by speaking about topics and issues that are important to the students and parents of your school, and showing students that this work is being conducted right in their own area. While nearby professors and experts are ideal, schools should consider using video conferencing to expand their reach to find the right speaker for their students.

Principals and teachers play a vital role in shaping the learning environment for their students. They are responsible for creating a safe, inclusive, and supportive atmosphere that promotes academic excellence and fosters a sense of belonging. One way that educators can enhance their school's culture is by shopping in the school's neighborhood, as touched on in Chapter 17.

By shopping in the school's neighborhood, school leaders can support local businesses. When they purchase goods and services from neighborhood merchants, they help to stimulate the economy around the school. This can help to create jobs and generate tax revenue that can be used to fund important school programs. Shopping in the school's neighborhood can also help build stronger ties with the community. When educators visit these businesses, they also have the opportunity to interact with business owners and workers and get to know them better. This can help to foster a sense of community and forge a positive relationship between the school and its surrounding neighborhoods.

Principals and teachers can gain a deep understanding of the culture by shopping in neighborhood local stores. In addition, by experiencing local customs and traditions, school leaders can create a more culturally responsive learning environment for their students. They can also tailor their programs and initiatives to better meet the needs of their students and their families. For example, if a school leader notices that a particular neighborhood lacks access to healthy food options, they may consider partnering with a local business to provide healthy snacks to students.

It is also vital to lead by example. By demonstrating their commitment to the community, school leaders set a positive example for their students and their families. This can help to create a culture of healthy engagement and inspire others to get involved in local initiatives.

What Now?

Many new administrators are unsure of how to interact with parents when just starting out. The truth is that parents can take first impressions and turn them into lasting perceptions. Here are a few ways to get started:

1. Get your first Coffee with the Principal on the schedule. Most school plans have a budget for parent interaction/involvement.

Use it to purchase traveler containers of fresh brewed coffee from a local coffee shop. Then stop by a local donut shop and pick up a few dozen donuts.

2. Take pictures of events like your Coffee with the Principal and post them on social media, tagging the school district and any parents who were in attendance.

3. Schedule a meeting with the dean of the local college's Department of Education. This is a great opportunity to discuss not only how your school can help with student-teacher placement, but also about the needs of the school and how the college can support your teachers, students, and families.

Chapter 19

One Call per Day

Principals get to make most of the really bad calls to parents from the school. Some of the more fun examples are:

- Disciplinary calls
- Detention notices
- Attendance concerns
- Suspensions/expulsions
- Academic concerns

For the most part, no parent likes to get a call from their child's principal. It is almost always bad news. That is, unless the principal flips the script.

Parents rarely get positive phone calls. However, when you share good news, you make the parent's and the child's day. These messages are most powerful when they are made to a parent who was called the week prior for a negative reason. While part of the job of a principal is to ensure that proper and fair consequences are given out, it is equally important to provide parents with encouraging feedback and progress. This helps to build the partnership and to gain an ally, not an adversary. These supportive calls can be made for just about any reason under the sun.

When a student's parent receives a praiseful phone call from the teacher or school leader, the student can become motivated to succeed in school. The parent may be more likely to encourage their child to work hard and take their studies seriously when they hear positive feedback from the school. A favorable communication can help to build productive relationships between the school, the student, and the parent. When the parent hears that their child is doing well in school, they may be more likely to view the school and the teacher in a appreciative light. This can help to build trust and improve communication between the school and the family.

When parents receive strong feedback about their child's progress, they may be more inspired to get involved in their child's education. They may attend parent-teacher conferences, volunteer at the school, or participate in school events. This increased involvement can lead to better academic outcomes for the student. When a student hears that their hard work and achievements are recognized and valued by the school, they may feel more confident in their abilities and more motivated both academically and behaviorally to continue to succeed.

Imagine if all staff members made one positive phone call home per day. That's potentially hundreds of warm-hearted messages per week. Think about all that positivity going out to your families and community.

Collaborative teacher-student relationships – evidenced by teachers' reports of low conflict, a high degree of closeness and support, and little dependency – have been shown to support students' adjustment to school, contribute to their social skills, promote academic performance, and foster students' resiliency (Battistich, Schaps, & Wilson, 2004; Birch & Ladd, 1997; Curby, Rimm-Kaufman, & Ponitz, 2009; Ewing & Taylor, 2009; Hamre & Pianta, 2001; Rudasill, Reio, Stipanovic, & Taylor, 2010).

Sending out positivity is important. As a principal, you will have days when you feel like the world is against you. It will seem like every interaction you have is negative and your students, teachers, staff members, and parents are out to get you. On those days, it is important to end with a complimentary phone call home for a student. While you might still feel beaten down by the day, take solace in the fact that you probably just made the day for one of your students and their parents.

Conversely, when schools only speak with parents when there are problems, it can lead to several challenges for both the students and the school community. First, it can create a negative perception of the school in the minds of parents. Parents may feel that the school only cares about their child when there is a problem, which can damage the relationship between the school and parents. When schools only call home for problems, it can decrease student motivation. Students may feel that their achievements and behaviors are not valued, which can lead to a lack of internal incentive to continue to work hard and succeed academically. It can also limit opportunities for students. Teachers may not have the opportunity to acknowledge and celebrate positive behavior and achievements, which can lead to a lack of recognition and missed opportunities for students. Continuously negative communication from school to home can stress relationships between teachers and students. Students may feel that teachers are only interested in disciplining them and not invested in their overall success. This can lead to strained relationships and a lack of trust between teachers and students. Ultimately, it can decrease parental involvement. Parents may not feel valued or involved in their child's education, which can lead to a lack of engagement in the school community.

What Now?

It is easy for new administrators to get bogged down in the weeds of school leadership and spend too much energy dealing with negativity. Taking the time to share positivity with a family can help provide some sunshine among the rain. Here is how to get started:

1. It can be hard not only to find the opportunity to make positive phone calls home, but also to decide whom to surprise with a call. Don't overthink it. A positive call home could be for something

big like moving up a grade level in a benchmark assessment or for holding a door open for a teacher.

2. Schedule time to speak with parents in your calendar. It is easy to get caught up in other things and convince yourself to skip the call for the day and make two tomorrow. Don't let that happen. Put 10 minutes on your calendar for this important communication.

3. Have an interpreter ready. Working in a school with English Language Learners means there is a good chance that many of the parents will speak a language other than English. Have a translator ready to support you. This is another reason why scheduling these calls is so important.

Chapter 20
Video Conferencing for All

For decades, teachers and principals relied on parents coming down to the school for a conference. This in-person conversation and collaboration was considered vital to the educational process. The COVID-19 pandemic changed how schools can communicate with their families, as in-person events were not an option.

Schools need to change their thinking on parent conferencing. Sure, it is nice for everyone to be in the same room; however, due to work schedules and other obligations, it can be difficult for parents to make a meeting with their child's teacher before or after school. We must remember that for some families, missing work means less money, and it is harder to put food on the table. We should not make families choose in this scenario, but give them options.

Parents who have several children in different schools or classrooms may find it hard to attend all the conferences. Some families may not have reliable transportation, and others may live in rural areas or have limited access to public transportation.

Video conferencing allows parents and teachers to conference without the need to be in the classroom at all. Work samples can be shared via a shared Google Drive or through email. The process is the same, the conversation is the same, the creation of an action plan can be the same. The only thing that is different is that the teacher and parents are not in the same location.

Video conferencing can also be used for student support meetings, where teachers, counselors, and administrators can discuss a student's academic or behavioral needs with parents. This can help to create a collaborative approach to supporting the student and can ensure that parents are informed and involved in the process.

School events, such as parent-teacher association meetings, school board meetings, and other community events can also be attended virtually through video conferencing. This can improve access and participation for parents who otherwise may miss in-person events due to scheduling or transportation barriers.

For students with special needs, video conferencing can be used for IEP meetings. These meetings are legally required to review a student's progress and develop an individualized plan for their academic and behavioral needs. Video conferencing can help to ensure that all necessary parties are able to participate in the process.

Video conferencing can be used for parent education sessions, such as workshops or seminars on topics such as school curriculum, technology use, or academic support strategies. These sessions can help to improve parent engagement in and knowledge of their child's education.

Using video conferencing also gives parents and teachers the option of conducting a conference in the evening or weekend if desired. While I am not advocating for teachers to work evenings and weekends, some teachers might not mind it, or actually prefer it.

Again, it is all about options. The more tools in your tool belt, the better.

What Now?

Before the COVID-19 pandemic, video conferencing was not widely used for parent conferences, staff meetings, and student-to-student projects. Consider keeping video conferencing as an option for communicating with more parents. While there might be some pushback, here are some ways to get started:

1. When discussing this idea with teachers, let them know that video conferences are not best practice for all students. There might only be a handful of conferences that this might work for.
2. Let parents know that video conferencing is an option. While you might not have many volunteers upfront, you will have some who will appreciate the flexibility and convenience.
3. Have your teachers practice. While this might sound unnecessary, conducting a conference with parents online is very different than in person. Teachers need to be ready to share work samples through email, shared drives, or a document camera.

Tales from the Principal's Desk

My middle school did not have a strong history of parental or community involvement. To be honest, the school was not a very welcoming place. Opportunities for parents to volunteer were few and far between. Furthermore, many of the parents at the school did not speak English, which became a barrier, as many of them had not felt welcomed by the school in the past. I knew that we had to improve this culture and increase inclusiveness, but I also did not want to bite off more than I could chew. These families were not ready to dive into volunteer activities in classrooms; we needed to cultivate and nurture relationships in order to build trust as well as a shared vision. First, we had to just physically get them to come into the school.

I tapped the person who I knew had the best chance of bringing in parents, my community liaison, Marie (not her real name). She was in charge of parent and community involvement as well as providing on-site translation services. Marie also lived in the community and knew some of the parents personally. I asked her to contact a few families and invite them to a morning coffee in the library. There would be no agenda, no speeches, just coffee.

A few days later, Marie appeared at my office door and let me know that she had five moms coming the following Wednesday morning. I took care of securing the coffee and she let me know that she would get some pastries. We were all set for our first parent coffee.

That morning, I waited in the library for our parents to arrive. They started coming in right after the first bell rang. Everyone poured themselves some coffee and chose a pastry. Then the conversation began. In Spanish. All of it. Not one word of English was spoken. I sat there, trying to recall my tenth-grade Spanish 2 class. I knew that B would come back to haunt me one day. I did a lot of smiling and nodding. Marie translated what she could for me without getting pulled too far out of the conversation. There was a lot of laughing going on. A lot.

I had scheduled the coffee for 30 minutes and as we were wrapping up, I thanked everyone for coming. Marie walked them out and I sat down thinking that this was a total disaster. I didn't get a word in. Not one word.

Later that day, I made my way over to Marie's office and asked her what she thought of the morning coffee. To my surprise, she said that everyone loved it and wanted to come back next week. I was thrilled with this information and told her to schedule the next coffee with the parents. Marie was already on it and said that everyone was going to bring a friend.

Next Wednesday came around quickly and we had twice the amount of people. I had the coffee ready, but this time, everyone brought homemade food to share. I hadn't had so much food pushed in front of me since, well, ever. That's when I realized that I had stumbled upon the secret sauce I was looking for.

That secret sauce was food.

Food brings people together. While many of the parents at my school did not feel that they had the skills to contribute to the academic programs we offered, they could cook like nobody's business. To this day, the best chilaquiles I've ever had were made by a parent at that school. We ended up having a standing coffee morning once a month. We averaged 35–40 parents each time, and each time everyone brought in food. We never had an agenda and most of the talking was in Spanish. I mostly sat back and enjoyed the food. After all, my goal was to bring parents into the school, and that goal was accomplished.

Even though that middle school was located in an economically disadvantaged area, I was lucky to have a retired chemistry professor from San Jose State University run an after-school science lab for my students. It was wonderful to have my students work with a professor who lived in the community, who looked like them and spoke Spanish like them. I wanted to utilize him even more, so I worked with him to plan our school's first career fair. We did our best to pull from local businesses, but the community was lacking in business opportunities. We were able to secure police officers and firefighters from local stations. However, I needed the "wow" factor. I wanted to bring in someone whom kids would go home and tell their parents about, such as the mayor, a professional athlete, or an astronaut.

I didn't get any of them, but I came close enough.

Our chemistry professor put me in touch with a former colleague of his. I gave this contact a call and was shocked when I found out where I was calling.

NASA.

More specifically, NASA AMES, located in Mountain View, California, 15 miles from my school. While I didn't call an astronaut, I did call someone who worked with astronauts. The scientist said he would be thrilled to come and speak with my students. He even said he'd bring along some items for them to look at.

It was AMAZING!

He mesmerized students with his stories from NASA. Once again, it was great for my students to see someone from their community achieve so much professionally. It gave them hope and allowed them to dream and wonder what was beyond their community.

Questions to Ask Yourself

- How effectively are we engaging and involving the community in our school's mission and initiatives? Reflect on the level of community engagement and involvement in the school.

Consider whether there are established mechanisms for two-way communication and collaboration with parents, local organizations, businesses, and other stakeholders. Assess the extent to which the community is actively involved in shaping the school's vision, programs, and initiatives. Think about strategies to enhance community engagement and create opportunities for meaningful participation.

- What are the strengths and needs of our community, and how can the school address them? Consider the unique abilities and challenges within the community surrounding the school. Account for the demographics, socioeconomic factors, and cultural diversity present in the community. Assess how well the school understands and responds to the specific needs of the community. Decide how the school can leverage community assets and resources to enhance educational opportunities and address any barriers to student success.

- How can the school build and strengthen partnerships with community organizations and agencies? Reflect on the existing partnerships between the school and community organizations or agencies. Analyze the nature and depth of these partnerships and their impact on supporting student learning and well-being. Assess the potential for collaboration with local businesses, nonprofit organizations, government agencies, and other community stakeholders. Ponder the strategies to establish new partnerships, leverage resources, and align community services and supports with the school's goals and priorities.

Pillar IV

Attendance

Chapter 21

Get to School, Ferris!

Growing up, I rarely missed a day of school. I maybe missed 2–3 days per year. I went to school with colds, a runny nose, coughs, and aches and pains. Missing a day of school was a big deal in my house. You had better be pretty sick in order to miss school. That meant a fever over 102 degrees. Anything below that was "just a cold" and I was told to tough it out.

Both my parents worked full-time, so missing a day of school when I was younger meant that one of them had to miss work. As I got older, I stayed home by myself, watching TV and resting up. Missing more than one day of school at a time was unheard-of in my family, until I came down with bronchitis and a double ear infection in 6th grade. I was out for two weeks.

I wasn't the type of kid to fake being sick, either. While I loved the movie *Ferris Bueller's Day Off*, I never thought to pull off my own epic ditch day.

When I was a classroom teacher, I never really thought about school attendance outside my own classroom. Only when I became an administrator did I begin to see the bigger picture. I was astonished to realize that so many children missed so many days of school. I had to learn all about SARB (student attendance review board) and truancy codes quickly.

I met with dozens of parents to explain that their child was considered truant. The excuses I heard from parents as to why their child wasn't attending school on a regular basis were as varied as the day is long. Here are a few of those excuses:

- They get sick a lot.
- They were tired because they were out late.
- They stay up too late playing video games.
- I thought they were coming to school.

While these families needed some tough love, there were other parents who came in with very different stories.

- We are living in our car and have to park across town at night where it is safe.
- We are living at a shelter because we are homeless.
- I had no one else to watch the baby while I was at work.
- The car broke down and we don't have the money to fix it.
- Bus passes are too expensive.
- Bullying.

The first group of families needed to understand the consequences of truancy and the lifelong impact of missing school. The second group needed help. For every Ferris Buller, there is a family in crisis. Ferris just needs to get to class. The other students need a more wraparound approach.

The most commonly accepted definition of school truancy is missing 10% or more of the school year. This usually equates to 18 days per school year. Interestingly enough, The US Department of Education does not determine truancy rates for schools. That is determined by state boards of education. The research is quite clear on the importance of school attendance. According to the US Department of Education, more than 20% of students in high school are chronically absent. More than 14% of students in middle school miss more than 10% of school per year.

Chronic absenteeism from school can have several negative consequences for the student later in life. Regularly missing school can lead to unfinished assignments, projects, and exams, which can negatively affect a student's academic performance. This, in turn, can limit their educational and career opportunities later in life. Truant students tend to have lower academic grades than their peers who attend school regularly. With lower grades, it will be much more difficult to be accepted into college or a vocational program. Without a good secondary education, it can be challenging to secure a decent job with good pay and benefits.

Truancy is one of the leading causes of dropping out of school. Students who miss a lot of school can become disengaged from their studies, feel discouraged, and ultimately choose to drop out of school altogether. Depending on the source, the dropout rate in the United States is somewhere between 5 and 7%.

Truant students are more likely to engage in dangerous behaviors such as drug and alcohol use, gang activity, and other criminal activities. These behaviors can result in legal consequences and negatively impact their social and emotional well-being. In addition, these behaviors can also lead to more absenteeism, making it more and more difficult to bring these students back into school.

Poverty increases the chances of a student becoming truant. In fact, truancy rates are three to four times higher in lower socioeconomic areas than in more affluent neighborhoods. Data indicates that students from low-income families are 2.4 times more likely to drop out of school than are children from middle-income families, and 10.5 times more likely than students from high-income families.

A lack of education paired with taking part in dangerous behaviors can lead to a lifetime of poverty. Truant students are more likely to struggle financially throughout their lives, making it challenging to break the cycle of poverty. It is vital the educators break this cycle and help students begin a new, healthier path to economic and social success. These challenges can make it difficult for students to attend school regularly, leading to truancy. A student's health can be greatly impacted by living in poverty, making them more susceptible to frequent illness and missing school. A lack of access to health care can also prevent a child from recovering from an illness quickly, leading to more missed days of school as well as spreading the illness to other siblings, causing them to miss school as well.

Students from low-income families may be required to help with earning money or looking after younger siblings, which can interfere with their ability to attend school regularly, especially if there is a baby or toddler. For many families, being late or missing a day of work will prevent them from putting food on the table. Parents and guardians must sometimes make the difficult decision between making money and having their child go to school.

I am grateful that my parents did not have to make that decision; however, I had friends who weren't so lucky.

Students living in poverty may face additional stressors that can impact their motivation to attend school. For example, if a student feels that they will not be able to attend college or secure a good job, they see less reason to attend school regularly. This, coupled with families not having the resources to provide their children with the emotional support they need to succeed in school, can result in students feeling disconnected from school and more likely to become truant.

Chapter 22

Get Butts in Seats

Some of the most important and inspiring advice that I have received during my career has come in some of the strangest forms. My philosophy on school improvement was born from one of those moments.

As a new principal, my districts had me connect with different administrators from around the district and county. On one particular day, all new principals in the district were asked to meet with the principal of a high school in a neighboring district, to walk the campus, and to get advice. I was excited for the opportunity as I was desperate to add some new tools to my principal toolbelt. I remember meeting with the principal in the cafeteria. There were about eight of us. Someone in the group asked him what was the most important aspect of the job of the principal. I will never forget what he said.

"My number-one job is to get butts in seats."

That's it. That's the job. Get butts in seats.

A school can have the finest Ivy League–educated teachers, the newest and most powerful technology, the most beautiful and welcoming campus, and the friendliest and most caring staff members – and it won't do any good if students are not at school with their butts in seats.

During my first year as a principal, I was hyper-focused on teacher development. I had many first-year teachers and they needed a lot of help with instructional delivery. They got the support they needed from me, the assistant principal, and our amazing instructional coach. Unfortunately, our formative and summative assessment scores weren't going up. The reason eluded me until that fateful day at the high school.

I needed to get butts in seats.

It was time to get tough on truancy.

We started with the data. Our daily attendance rate was 92%. You might be thinking, that's not bad. Truth be told, 92% was the state average, so my school was right in line with the masses. But it wasn't good enough. We knew the research, especially with the community we served. If we wanted students to learn at higher levels, we needed to increase attendance rates.

We started with letters to parents, educating them on the importance of daily school attendance. We explained the connection between attending school every day and high school graduation rates as well as college acceptance rates. We printed these letters every month, in addition informing parents if their child was considered truant or at-risk for being truant. Parent conferences were set up for the parents of students who were considered truant.

The vast majority of time, these meetings were amicable. Most of the parents needed help in either logistically getting their child to school or with motivating them to get to school. These were caring parents who just needed guidance.

Then there were the other meetings.

These were contentious. Keep in mind that many of these meetings were only held after two or three attempts to bring in the parents. For these special cases, I called for backup.

Literally.

I had my school resource officer (SRO) attend these meetings. They were not there to intimidate parents, but to show how important this conversation was to the future of their child. Only after things got heated did they start to lay down the law. Santa Clara

County was one of the first counties to get tough on truancy. More specifically, they got tough on the parents of truant children. The SRO would explain that laws had been passed holding parents accountable for their child's school attendance. Parents could be incarcerated for up to 30 days if their child was habitually truant. For most parents, this was enough to get them to realize that things needed to change. I had a few parents, however, who continued to be defiant.

These families had to attend a student attendance review board (SARB) meeting. These meetings were held at the district office with the director of student services, the principal of the school, the parents, and a school resource officer. The seriousness of the situation was reiterated to the family. Contracts were written up letting parents know the potential consequences of their child's continuing to miss school.

I had one family that did not pull it together. Unfortunately for them, the district attorney was sick and tired of students missing school. His judgment was swift and serious. First, the father went to jail for 30 days. Once he was released, the mom went in for 30 days.

That fixed it.

Now, the rumors about this outcome ran rampant through our school community. Usually, I would work hard to put a stop to such rumors, but I let this one breathe. We were taking a hard stance on truancy and I wanted everyone to know.

We did not let up on our phone calls and letters. We conducted home visits, met parents at their place of work, and followed up with support. If a parent couldn't pay for a bus pass for their child, we secured one for them. If the students needed a ride to work, we found them a carpool. If they needed a buddy to walk to school with, we paired them up.

In one year, our school went from 92% average daily attendance to 98% average daily attendance, the best in the district. Furthermore, with the increase of daily attendance, we saw an increase in academic achievement across the board.

Get butts in seats. It works.

What Now?

Attendance is one of, if not the most important indicators of school success. However, it is an aspect of school data that many school leaders don't know how to access or what to do once it is obtained. Here is how to get started:

1. Ensure that there is a way to pull attendance data quickly and easily. Daily or even weekly attendance reports rarely make it to the principal's desk. Start requesting these reports and get to know your most absentee students.
2. Along with monitoring full-day absences, start to track tardies, late arrivals, and early pullouts. Understanding these details will help you frame future conversations with parents.
3. Include truancy research with your newsletters and blogs. Letting parents know you are serious about daily attendance will help you set the foundation for change.

Chapter 23
Conducting Home Visits

I know what you're thinking: *There is no way that I have time to conduct home visits.*

Yes, you do.

Remember, one of the most effective ways to improve a school is to improve attendance. Think back to our first pillar – instruction – and remember that after I collected student engagement data from every classroom on campus, I discovered that students were truly engaged only 11 minutes per every 54-minute period.

The same can be said for principals.

Think about your day. How much of it are you spending on tasks that are truly making a difference? Completing paperwork, getting your third cup of coffee, or redrafting the seventh edition of your school safety plan is not going to make a huge impact on student achievement. Taking your attendance problem seriously will make a big impact on student achievement.

I have found that conducting home visits for students who are habitually truant is the best way to get them back on track. Here's how you do it.

It is important to call ahead to the family to let them know you would like to stop by to talk. I have found that it is best to give them an hour or two to allow them the time to straighten up their house if they want. The families I have worked with in the past have taken great pride in the appearance of their home, no matter their living situation.

When we arrived at the home, we would knock and identify ourselves. When the door opened, we would greet the parent and again state the purpose for the visit. Most of the time, the conversation would happen in the doorway, but now and again, we would be welcomed inside for coffee.

We would always come prepared with information to support the parent. When applicable, we would connect the family with outside agencies for counseling or other support such as food banks, drug counseling, or transportation solutions. In all my years of conducting home visits, I never had a family be unappreciative of us visiting their home. Many of the families we serve are struggling to just make ends meet. They don't know which way to turn or whom to ask for help. It is important that they understand the school is there not only to help their child get an education, but to help the whole family as well.

If no one was home at the time of the visit, we always left a note letting the family know that we were there, and asking them to please call the school or stop by at their earliest convenience.

These visits also allowed us to see into the lives of our students once they leave school each day. I was concerned when I saw the living conditions of some of the families we worked with. Too many families were living in varying degrees of poverty. Sometimes we saw trash all over the floor, couches converted to beds, and unsanitary conditions in the kitchen. These realities gave us a sense of perspective. Having a child forget their backpack at home on a regular basis isn't so important when you see that their family of six lives in a converted garage with little fresh air or heat.

Conducting home visits usually had a big impact on families and we saw an immediate turnaround when it came to school attendance. However, there was another side to conducting these visits that helped us to get to the root cause of some of the attendance issues. On some occasions, we visited addresses that were no longer inhabited by the family we were hoping to meet with. It is not uncommon for families to move without telling the school, especially if it is out of the school's boundary. While it is easy to understand why a family would not notify the school upon moving (so as not to disrupt their child's schooling and friendships) it can create situations that affect school attendance. Moving further away from the school means some families will have more difficulty getting their child to school.

When such a situation was uncovered, we worked with the family to enroll their child in their new neighborhood school. We did make some exceptions, especially if it was late in the school year and if the truancy was cleaned up. We worked with families in the best interest of the child. Whatever that was, that was the direction we went.

One aspect of home visits that I have found to be vital is to bring along teachers when possible. I worked with many teachers over the years who routinely sent students to the office for not having a pencil, homework, or their textbook. I will tell these teachers time and time again that these were minor issues compared to the bigger picture and that we should celebrate that some of our students were coming to school at all. It didn't help. I insisted that they come with me to conduct a home visit on one of their students during their prep period. I told them I would gladly take their class at another time to even out the prep time. Sadly, some teachers never took me up on my offer. Some finally did, however, and it permanently changed their perspective.

We all have seen the images and videos of families living in poverty on the news. However, it is very different when it is being experienced in real life by someone whom you know personally. When I visited homes with teachers, we were most always asked to come inside. Entering the house, I watched the teachers take it all in: the mess, the dirtiness, the smell, and cramped quarters. At that moment, a missing pencil or homework assignment no longer seemed so important.

Research published by Johns Hopkins School of Education in 2018 found, on average, schools that systematically implemented home visits experienced decreased rates of chronic absenteeism and increased rates of English Language Arts and math proficiency.

In one district studied, schools that regularly conducted home visits saw a 5% increase in students scoring proficient on the ELA test, compared with 3% for schools that did not conduct home visits or that did so with fewer than 10% of students' families. In addition, research found students attending a school that conducted home visits with at least 10% of students' families were less likely to be chronically absent (Arundel, 2022).

What Now?

Most new administrators come to the position without ever conducting a home visit. Furthermore, many administrators finish out their careers without ever visiting a student's home. Let's change that, starting with you.

1. Make a home visit schedule. Putting tasks on your schedule is a theme in this book. The job of a principal is nonstop and full of unexpected detours and surprises. If you don't put something on the calendar, there is a good chance it won't happen.
2. Know your purpose for the home visit before getting in the car. Conducting a home visit just to check off a box will not serve you or your students in the least. Know your purpose for going.
3. If applicable, inform the office that handles translators that you will be conducting home visits throughout the year and will need translation support. This will help you be prepared to make the most of the conversations you will have at each home.

Chapter 24

Creating Attendance Plans That Work

Every year, schools rewrite plans to address attendance concerns. These plans usually include different incentives, such as attendance awards, tangible prizes, recognition assemblies, and students' names in the monthly newsletter. Every year, we reword this same plan and attendance rates stay just about the same. Hours are spent on these plans that don't make a difference in the lives of children who need to be in school. Habitually absent or tardy students usually stay that way with attendance plans that don't address the real issue. These plans are just a Band-Aid. They treat symptoms, not the problems.

School attendance plans fail for a variety of reasons. If parents, students, or staff members do not fully understand or support the attendance plan, they may not be motivated to follow it. Attendance plans require resources, such as staff time and funding, to be successful. If schools do not have the necessary resources to implement the plan effectively, it may not succeed. This can lead to frustration and disengagement from stakeholders. It is important to create plans where the desired goal is within stretchable reach. Your school will need to experience short goal wins in increments. Creating a goal that is too ambitious can backfire.

Attendance plans require consistent and sustained effort to be effective. If schools do not follow through on implementing the plan or do not consistently enforce attendance policies, they may not be able to improve attendance rates.

A strong school attendance plan typically includes several components. An attendance plan should clearly define its goals and objectives, such as reducing chronic absenteeism rates or increasing overall attendance rates. This helps to ensure that everyone involved in the plan is working toward a common goal. It should be based on a comprehensive analysis of attendance data, including identifying patterns and trends in absenteeism rates, as well as the reasons for absences. This can help schools to target their interventions and supports more effectively.

Attendance plans should include multitiered interventions that address the root causes of absenteeism and provide targeted support to students and families who need it. This may include strategies such as mentoring programs, attendance incentives, and family outreach. Consistent and clear communication is essential when implementing a new schoolwide attendance plan. The plan should include clear, consistent communication with students, families, and staff about the importance of attendance and the supports available to them. This can help to build buy-in and ensure that everyone is aware of the plan and their role in supporting it.

The attendance plan should include ongoing monitoring and evaluation to assess its effectiveness and identify areas for improvement. This may include tracking attendance data, conducting surveys or focus groups with stakeholders, and making adjustments to the plan as needed. Your attendance plan should involve collaboration with community partners, such as local agencies and organizations, to provide additional supports and resources to students and families. This can help to build a stronger network of support and increase the success of the attendance plan.

You are not going to get students who are habitually truant to come to school on the promise of an attendance certificate.

Better attendance rates come from changing the culture of your school.

Many students in middle and high school miss countless days of instruction due to lack of engagement. They simply don't care about missing school, as they find school boring. We can't expect students to sit on the edge of their seat, fixated on every word we say. Students need to be exposed to exciting, engaging instruction that puts them in the driver's seat of their own learning. Seating students in rows and talking at them isn't going to motivate them to come to school. They are more likely to come to school when they are excited about being in class or being able to spend time with their favorite teacher. They don't mind missing school if they believe that their teacher(s) don't believe in them.

Students also need to understand why they need to come to school. What is in it for them? Recognizing their goals and tailoring education programs to meet their needs is essential. They need to see how attending school will help them achieve their dreams, whether that is attending college, getting a job as a construction worker, or going into the military.

Depending on your district, you may or may not have a school nurse. I'm not talking about a para-educator who is posing as a school nurse, but a certified RN.

It is important to keep in mind that teachers and administrators are not medical professionals and should never offer parents or guardians medical advice or attempt to diagnose a child. It might seem far-fetched that this would occur in schools, but it happens constantly. While educators should stay away from providing any medical direction, school nurses are able to engage parents in discussions around health and medical concerns. School nurses can be a very important member of your front office team and assist parents in obtaining support.

It is also important to note that nurses can spot needs that educators might overlook. The need for glasses or special shoes can go unnoticed by administrators, but easily acknowledged right away by the school nurse. They can also be instrumental in helping families obtain free glasses that can help prevent students from missing school due to frequent headaches from squinting at the board. They can also support parents in connecting them to free clinics, doctors, behavioral therapists, and counselors in the community.

Home visits need to be an integral of a school's attendance plan. As we discussed in the previous chapter, they are one of the most powerful tools in an educator's tool belt. A home visit can open the eyes of an educator into the real world of a child when they leave school in the afternoon. These visits also convey to the parents a deep sense of respect and caring about their child. That understanding can be the tipping point for a child to come to school more often as a deeper connection between the school and home has been established. Showing up at a home with an attendance liaison or social worker can also make a powerful statement. For your more chronic cases, having a police officer present can really open the eyes of a family to the truancy issue.

Let's talk about soap for a minute. I know what you are thinking. Really . . . soap. Yes, soap!

I've been lucky to be able to visit many different schools in many different districts, across many different states. I have walked through countless classrooms, gyms, cafeterias, hallways, and playgrounds. These are mostly all well maintained, clean, and safe for children. However, if you want to see true commitment to creating a safe and healthy environment, check out the bathrooms. I know, gross, right? However, as gross as it seems, you can learn a lot about a school by checking out the cleanliness of the bathrooms. There is one item that I specifically look for when checking out a school's bathroom. I check to see if there is soap.

Any doctor will tell you that the best way to cut down on illnesses is to ensure that hands are being washed. By cutting down on illnesses, schools can increase attendance rates. Sadly, on many visits to school, I find that soap is either missing from the bathrooms altogether or they are using powdered soap from decades long past. While the powdered version is cheaper than the liquid antibacterial soap, it is also less effective to getting hands clean. Can we all make the investment in our students and schools by installing proper soap dispensers?

Schools can play an important role in promoting good hygiene habits by teaching students proper handwashing techniques, including washing hands with soap and water for at least 20 seconds, scrubbing all surfaces of the hands, and drying thoroughly. Posters and signs in restrooms can serve as a visual reminder for students.

Provide hand sanitizer stations throughout the school, especially in high-traffic areas like the cafeteria and entrances. Teachers can remind students to use hand sanitizer after coughing or sneezing, after using shared equipment or supplies, and before and after eating.

Schools can also teach students tissue etiquette by covering their mouths and noses with a tissue when coughing or sneezing, and to dispose of used tissues properly in a trash can. Teachers can also remind students to avoid touching their face, mouth, or nose with their hands.

To bring in the home–school connection, schools can educate students on the importance of personal hygiene, including showering or bathing regularly, wearing clean clothes, and brushing teeth twice a day. Teachers can also remind students to avoid sharing personal items like combs, brushes, and hats that might spread germs and lice.

While it might seem like someone else's job, keeping restrooms and classrooms clean and well maintained, providing adequate supplies like soap and paper towels, and encouraging students to report any issues or concerns is the responsibility of a school leader.

For elementary students, attendance is more of a parent issue than a student issue. Work with your parent community to inform them of the benefits of daily school attendance as well as the repercussions of poor attendance. As we all know, the effects can be long-lasting. Many times, parents don't realize the severity of the situation. One trick I have learned along the way is to put the parent of a child with poor attendance in charge of something at the school. It doesn't have to be big, but if mom or dad is coming to school to help out, chances are the child is coming to school, too.

Too many attendance plans focus on awards. Specifically, the Perfect Attendance Award. Here's the thing . . . kids get sick.

Let me rephrase . . . all kids get sick.

Creating a culture where we are encouraging students to come to school sick can not only drastically affect their ability to get better quickly but also cause other students and teachers to get sick and miss school. These awards should not be a part of any attendance plans.

While a cold shouldn't always stop a child from coming to school, the flu should. Furthermore, the child shouldn't feel like they are being punished by staying home and resting in order to get back to school as soon as possible.

While these attendance plan recommendations seem simple, they are effective. There is no need to create a 200-page attendance manifesto. Instead, go out and conduct some home visits. You'll get better results.

What Now?

Creating a strong and productive attendance plan needs to be a priority. Again, many new administrators have little to no experience in writing and following through on an attendance plan. Here's how to get started:

1. Survey your staff to find out what systems of support are currently in place, and learn how these supports are being accessed by parents.
2. Start an attendance committee composed of teachers and parents. The best plans are created with a variety of stakeholders at the table.
3. Inspect at least one bathroom a day for soap. I'm not joking.

Chapter 25
Holding Parents Accountable

There will be times where you will have to acknowledge that your superpowers as a principal will not do much to get parents on board with ensuring that their child comes to school every day. There are limits to the job. While we can be persistent, we can't go above and beyond our role. Luckily, there are individuals out there who can take what you have started and expand on it.

Bringing in social workers and child advocates can be a major help in improving a child's school attendance. There are many factors that can contribute to poor attendance, including family issues, health problems, transportation barriers, and academic struggles. Social workers can play a key role in improving a child's school attendance by addressing these underlying issues and providing targeted interventions and support.

Social workers can work with families to identify and address the root causes of chronic absenteeism. This might involve connecting families with resources such as counseling services, health care providers, or transportation assistance. Social workers can also work with families to develop strategies for improving attendance, such as setting achievable goals and creating a supportive environment at home.

Social workers can also work directly with students to address academic and behavioral issues that may be contributing to absenteeism. This might involve providing one-on-one counseling or coaching, connecting students with academic support services, or working with teachers to develop targeted interventions. Social workers can also help students develop the social and emotional skills needed to succeed in school, such as problem-solving, self-regulation, and relationship building.

Parenting classes are usually available through local agencies for free or a nominal fee. Parenting classes can play an important role in improving a child's school attendance by providing parents with the knowledge and skills needed to create a supportive and nurturing home environment that promotes academic success.

Parenting classes can provide parents with valuable information and resources about the importance of school attendance, as well as strategies for addressing common challenges that can lead to absenteeism. This might include information about the impact of absenteeism on academic achievement, the importance of creating a routine and consistent schedule, and strategies for addressing common health and family issues that can contribute to absenteeism.

Another topic covered in most parenting classes is how to create a supportive and nurturing home environment that promotes academic success. This might include strategies for setting expectations and boundaries, building strong relationships with children, promoting positive behavior and self-regulation, and developing effective communication and problem-solving skills.

Parents must understand that they are not alone in this journey. Remember, more than 20% of students in high school are chronically absent and more than 14% in middle school upwards of 10% of school per year. Parenting classes can provide parents with an opportunity to connect with other parents and build a supportive community. This can help parents feel more connected to their children's school and the broader community, and can provide them with valuable support and resources as they work to promote school attendance and academic success.

Parents need to understand the importance of their role in supporting their child's academic success, and the school can provide them with strategies for promoting academic achievement and engagement. This might include strategies for helping children with homework, creating a positive learning environment at home, and supporting children's interests and passions. Parenting classes can help struggling guardians get back in control of their home and work with their child to get them to return to and attend school on a regular basis.

One of the most important aspects of a social worker's role is that they can collaborate with your school, community organizations, and other stakeholders to develop comprehensive attendance improvement plans. This might involve conducting needs assessments, identifying best practices, and developing targeted interventions that address the unique needs of each student and family.

It is important to note that when a child is truant, there might be, either knowingly or unknowingly, laws being broken. When the truancy gets severe enough it is time to bring in your School Resource Officer (SRO).

Truancy is considered a status offense, which means that it is an offense that is only illegal because of the age or status of the individual involved. Principals should become familiar with these laws. Laws may be different from state to state, but there are some laws that can be considered more universal.

Failure to Comply with Compulsory Education Laws

Every state in the United States has laws that require children to attend school until a certain age, typically 16 or 18 years old. Parents or guardians who fail to ensure that their child attends school can be charged with a crime, such as truancy, contributing to the delinquency of a minor, or neglect.

Educational Neglect

Educational neglect refers to the failure of a parent or guardian to ensure that their child receives a suitable education. If a child is consistently absent from school, it can be considered educational neglect, and the parent or guardian can be charged with a crime.

Child Endangerment

If a child's chronic truancy leads to them engaging in dangerous activities or puts them in harm's way, the parent or guardian can be charged with child endangerment.

Complicity

If a parent or guardian knowingly allows their child to skip school or encourages their child to skip school, they can be charged with complicity.

It should never be the goal for school officials to be punitive toward parents when involving the police. The goal of truancy laws and related crimes is not to punish parents or their children, but to ensure that children receive the education they need to succeed in life. The criminal justice system can work with schools and community organizations to address the root causes of truancy and provide support and resources to families who are struggling.

The type and severity of punishment that parents can face for their child's truancy vary depending on the state and the specific circumstances. Parents may be fined for their child's unexcused absences from school. The amount of the fine can vary, but it is usually a few hundred dollars. In some cases, parents may be required to perform community service as a result of their child's truancy. Parents may be placed on probation, which means they must meet certain conditions, such as ensuring their child attends school regularly.

In extreme cases, parents can be sentenced to jail time for their child's truancy, as was the case for my extreme parent. This is rare and typically reserved for cases where parents are repeat offenders or have been found guilty of educational neglect. If a parent is consistently unable to ensure that their child attends school regularly, they may face losing custody of their child.

Again, the goal is not to let things progress this far, but to get families the help they need in order for their children to be successful in school. You will be faced with situations where you will need to bring in social workers and police officers to assist you in working with the families. In some cases, as mentioned, parents might face some pretty tough consequences. Remember, when the going gets tough, always advocate for the child.

That is always the right path.

What Now?

Educators need to be never-ending supporters of the students they work with. At times, that can mean taking a hard stance against the parents of a student. This can be very challenging for new administrators. Here is how to get started:

1. Start to document everything. Sending truancy letters, arranging phone calls and conferences, and speaking to social workers, SARB officers, and law enforcement all need to be documented so that you can show there has been a concerted effort to work with the family.
2. Know the law. Educators are not lawyers; however, it is important that administrators know their local/state truancy laws and whom to contact at the district office or police department if support is needed.
3. If the school doesn't have a social worker, work with local agencies to secure one when needed.

Tales from the Principal's Desk

Increasing your school's average daily attendance is not easy. There is no quick fix or magic bullet. It takes dedication, time, and follow-through. Parents need to know that you mean business. I let them know, one phone call at a time.

While most of the parents that I worked with would notify the school when their child was out of school, we had some that never called in. To me, this was unacceptable. They knew the rules. Yet, they had been getting away with it for years without any consequences. Meanwhile, their child was performing poorly in school due to their truant status and missing so much class time that they were far behind the other students.

My office staff spent over an hour each day trying to track down these parents so that we knew that their child was safe at home or somewhere being supervised and not roaming the neighborhood. Most of these families only had cell phones. This meant that they could see who was calling them before choosing to answer the call or not. Most times, they either hung up on us or let it go to voicemail. This game was wasting valuable time for the office staff. We knew that there must be a better way.

There was.

Robocalls!

Well, sort of.

Most schools have a system that will send a recorded message out to parents. Most of the time, this system is used to make general, schoolwide announcements about open houses, late buses, fundraisers, or to remind parents about an early day. But, did you know that with most of these systems, you can send specific messages to specific parents? You can! And it can be fun!

I recorded two different messages. The first message was to inform parents that their child was absent from school and that we had not yet heard from them to provide an excuse. The second message was to inform parents that their child has been late to one or more of their classes that day and to please speak with them about getting to class on time.

They went like this:

"Hello. This is Dr. Franklin from _____ School. The purpose of this call is to inform you that your child has an unexcused absence from school today. Please call the school at _____ to indicate the reason for their absence. Thank you."

"Hello. This is Dr. Franklin from _____ School. The purpose of this call is to inform you that your child has been late to one or more of their classes today. When your child is late to class, they are not only missing out on important instruction, but disrupting the entire class when they walk in the door. Please speak to your child about the importance of getting to class on time. Thank you."

Then, I set up our online attendance system to email me reports at the start of the school day, as well as for each period, so that I could see who was absent without a parental excuse and who was late to a class period. When I started this plan, there were routinely 30 to 40 names on these reports. I set my messaging system to send out the appropriate message to the parents of the students on that list. For the tardy students, it was just a message to inform them that their child was late to class. No action was needed. For students who were absent without an excuse, the system called parents every 20 minutes until they called back.

No. I didn't make any friends out of these parents by doing this. But the truth was that I wasn't trying to. I wanted to frustrate them and get them fired up, just as my teachers were when their students routinely walked into class late.

We did, however, see a decrease in student tardiness and absenteeism immediately. Consistency was the key. I pulled reports and set up calls each day. I also had the message translated for our Spanish-speaking families.

The teachers took notice as well. One of their biggest complaints to me was the frequent interruptions that occurred when a student walked in the door late for the first period. Everyone would turn around to see who was walking in the door late. Teachers would have to give directions again to ensure that everyone understood what to do.

When a student arrives late to class, they can disrupt the flow of the lesson and distract other students. The teacher may need to pause the lesson to accommodate the late student, which can be frustrating and result in lost instructional time. Depending on the circumstances, a student arriving late may cause a disturbance as they enter the classroom, such as by opening and closing the door loudly or making noise as they move to their seat. When a student arrives late, the teacher may need to shift their attention away from the lesson to address the tardiness, which can disrupt their focus and make it more difficult to deliver the lesson effectively. If a student is habitually late to class, the teacher feels that the student is not prioritizing their education or taking the class seriously. This can be frustrating for the teacher, who may feel that they are not able to help the student succeed.

Passing periods before we implemented this new system looked like free-for-alls, with many students paying little to no attention to the tardy bells. Students routinely walked into the class 3–4 minutes late. Teachers were fed up, frustrated, and looking for solutions. The solution came in the form of these automated calls. Our most frequent offenders were getting several messages sent home every day.

Don't get me wrong. It was not all sunshine and rainbows. I had some very angry parents finally call the school or come down in person to yell at me and to demand that I stop calling them when their child was late to a class. My answer was very clear to them. I promised to keep calling until their child got to class on time. I would explain that by drawing a line in the sand on this issue, we were teaching our students that punctuality was important. When they were older and working, they would be expected to show up on time, each and every day. Missing work or routinely coming in late would result in getting fired and lead to increased hardships.

This plan did make a difference. It did get butts in seats. And it did put our community on notice that this school took attendance very, very seriously.

Questions to Ask Yourself

- What is our current attendance rate, and how does it compare to benchmarks or targets? Reflect and consider whether the attendance rate meets the desired standards for regular school attendance. Assess whether there are specific subgroups or grade levels with lower attendance rates that require targeted interventions.
- What are the underlying factors contributing to low attendance rates? Think about the potential factors and take into account individual, family, and community factors that may affect student attendance. Assess whether there are systemic issues, such as school climate, engagement, or transportation, that may influence attendance patterns. Reflect on any barriers to attendance that need to be addressed.
- What strategies and supports can we implement to improve attendance rates? Consider proactive measures such as implementing attendance campaigns, developing positive reinforcement systems, and fostering relationships with families and community partners. Assess whether there is a need for targeted interventions, such as mentoring programs, attendance incentives, or family support services, to address specific attendance challenges.

Pillar V

Culture

Chapter 26
Culture Is Everything

There are many different quotes that I turn to when I need to put things into perspective. Here are a few of my favorites:

Culture eats strategy for breakfast.
—Peter Drucker

Earn trust, earn trust, earn trust. Then you can worry about the rest.
—Seth Godin

The most dangerous phrase in the language is: We've always done it this way.
—Rear Admiral Grace Hopper

School culture is the connective tissue that holds a great school together. A school's culture speaks to every pillar in this book: leadership, instruction, community, and attendance. School culture is a critical factor in promoting student success. A favorable school environment can help students feel more connected to their school, teachers, and peers, which can lead to better academic outcomes.

A welcoming school culture can help reduce student absenteeism. Students who feel like they belong in their school are more likely to attend school regularly. A supportive school that values inclusivity and encourages student involvement can help reduce absenteeism. Schools that prioritize equity and comprehensiveness in their environment can help ensure that all students feel valued and supported, regardless of their backgrounds or circumstances; emphasizing respect, responsibility, and kindness can help promote positive student behavior and reduce disciplinary problems.

Teachers who work in schools with positive environments are more likely to feel supported, valued, and engaged in their work. This, in turn, can lead to better teacher retention rates and increased job satisfaction. There is no better indicator of a school that doesn't have a favorable culture than teacher turnover.

As we begin to discuss school *culture*, let's ensure that we are not confusing it with *climate*.

Climate refers to the overall mood at the school right now. Think of it as something that can go up or down depending on current actions or factors. The climate of a school can be drastically different on a Monday morning than on a Friday afternoon, solely because it's the beginning or end of the week. Climate can also be affected by union negotiations, pay increases, or hitting a fundraising goal. These are all factors that can have an impact on the school in the short term. Schools and districts can go through stressful and contentious union negotiations, but once an agreement has been reached, the tension eases and the side effects are not long lasting.

School culture refers to the values, beliefs, customs, practices, traditions, and social behaviors that characterize a particular school community. It encompasses the attitudes and behaviors of students, teachers, administrators, and staff, as well as the physical environment and overall atmosphere of the school. A school's culture can be affected by many things: being in disrepair for years on end, dealing with a lack of a disciplinary structure, or having poor working conditions and low pay.

School culture can include elements like the school's mission and vision, policies and procedures, the relationships between staff and students, the level of student engagement, and the overall climate of the school. It can be shaped by a variety of factors, such as the school's history, location, and student demographics, and the leadership and management style of the administration.

I have seen many principals spend hours on end and thousands of dollars trying to change the culture of the school, but in reality, they are only scratching the surface of the school's climate. Too often, principals make this mistake, and are left frustrated.

A school's culture can't be changed by the following:

- Snacks in the staff room
- A cute note in a teacher's box
- A certificate of appreciation

These approaches to fixing the culture of a school are used way too often. While everyone likes to walk into the staff room to get some tasty treats, doing so will not change how they feel about the school, their students, or you.

This concept reminds me of the movie *Gladiator* with Russell Crowe. Toward the middle of the movie, the new Roman Emperor, Commodus, has games in the Colosseum on a daily basis for 100 days. While these games might make the citizens of Rome happy while they are there, it doesn't change the fact that the city was corrupt, and that the vast majority of people were living in squalor.

Changing the climate of a school is easy. Changing the culture is difficult.

It takes time, energy, out-of-the-box thinking, and commitment. but it can be done.

To accomplish this, school leaders must consider many different variables, including equity and inclusion, physical safety, public opinion, and collaboration between all stakeholders. To be clear, this does not mean having a multicultural night, a safety drill, and a one-off school advisory council meeting.

A school's culture is often developed over a long period of time and is deeply ingrained in the organization's structure and processes. Thus, it can be difficult to alter the culture, as it requires a significant effort to shift the attitudes and behaviors of staff members, and may require revisions to the school's systems and processes. Staff members may be resistant to reform, particularly if they feel that their status or job security is threatened. They may also be skeptical of new initiatives, particularly if they have seen previous attempts at revamping fail. I have had many teachers tell me that they are going to wait this one out because they have already "been there, done that."

Changing school culture requires strong leadership support and a clear vision for the future. Without this, staff members may not feel motivated or engaged in the process of moving their school forward. Furthermore, there may be structural barriers that make it difficult to modify the school's culture, such as existing policies, procedures, or systems that reinforce the existing culture. These barriers may be difficult to overcome, particularly if they are deeply entrenched in the organization over time.

Effective communication is critical to reworking school culture. Without clear communication about the reasons for change, the benefits of change, and the steps being taken to implement change, teachers and staff members may not understand or support the new direction.

Reform measures won't occur overnight. It is a long process that will ebb and flow.

Longtime country music singer Crystal Gayle might have said it best: "You are either in it for the long haul, or you're not."

One of the most interesting and polarizing concepts in education that has popped up in recent years is the notion of "toxic positivity," which views negative emotions as inherently bad. Instead, positivity and happiness are compulsively pushed, and authentic human emotional experiences are denied, minimized, or invalidated.

Toxic positivity has made its way into every profession over the past several years, but nowhere is it as prevalent as in education. Social media has given a worldwide platform for so-called "edu celebrities" to share messages of toxic positivity with educators everywhere. These messages do not reflect the real feelings of teachers and administrators who are working directly with students on a daily basis and feel the stress, heartbreak, and pressure of the work. Furthermore, the messages that are blasted over social media tend to be vague and without any real merit.

For example, I participated in a Twitter chat where an "edu celebrity" was moderating the questions and responding to participants. A teacher asked a question about best ways to engage with a reluctant learner who was withdrawn and standoffish. The "edu celebrity" gave a vague answer, not tied to research or best practice. When pressed for more information by the teacher, the reply that was given was: "Be more awesome."

Yes. "Be more awesome."

Educators need to share best practices, rooted in research, that are tied to results, not messages that invoke toxic positivity.

No one enters the field of education as a means to make lots of money. The starting salaries for other professions that require similar education (a college degree, plus additional certification) are often the same as the top of the pay scale for a teacher. I recently came across the starting salary of a teacher in Colorado. A new teacher in Colorado can expect to make around $35,000 a year in 2022. Keep in mind that Zillow indicates that the average monthly rent for a one-bedroom apartment in the Denver area is $1,604. Let's also keep in mind that the starting pay at McDonalds is currently between $15 and $18 per hour. A full-time, starting employee at McDonalds can expect to make around $34,320 per year. No, teachers don't work for the income, but they shouldn't be forced to make a salary that is only slightly better than minimum wage. Teachers need to be paid like the professionals they are. Stop selling T-shirts that try to make this disparity acceptable as there are thousands of teachers out there who are having trouble paying their bills. Principals need to be aware of this reality and not minimize it.

We have all seen the perfect classroom and front-office pictures posted on social media. I call them IG- or Pinterest-ready classrooms, as these pictures are only posted to show everyone how amazing a teacher's classroom looks.

That is the key: how it looks.

Most of these pictures have a fatal flaw: They are not functional. They also don't look "perfect" five minutes after students enter the classroom. Teachers need to see functionality, not perceived physical perfection. Furthermore, classroom decor can also reflect inequalities in budgets between schools and teachers. The new teacher in Colorado won't be able to afford to purchase additional decor for their classroom as they will have enough trouble making their rent payment. Again, principals need to be aware of this reality.

All students deserve to be greeted at the door by their teacher with "good morning" and a smile. Students need to feel welcome in their classroom and comfortable with their surroundings. Classrooms need to be places of positive vibes. However, the trend of the super-long dance routine or individual greetings is not needed or realistic. In speaking to some of the teachers who have posted videos of themselves on IG and Twitter greeting each student individually with their own personalized handshake, many of them have indicated that they stopped this practice after a week or two as it got to be too cumbersome and time consuming. One also must ask the questions, "Who is filming this and why was this filmed in the first place?" The answer is that these videos are self-serving and are perfect for social media, but are another example of toxic positivity in schools.

The notion of toxic positivity has been long discussed in regard to social media. Recently, Instagram has been under fire for being harmful to children as it showcases an unrealistic notion of perfection and what a child should look or act like. The same principle applies to toxic positivity in education with intricate and unnecessary dance routines and unrealistic notions of perfection.

Don't get me wrong. Schools need positivity. However, educators shouldn't bury their heads in the sand and pretend that everything is all right. Educators are facing real problems, on the student side and the personal side. Demands upon teachers are growing every year. No longer able to just teach content, teachers are now also serving as counselors, statisticians, nurses, and surrogate parents. They are doing this all on a teacher's salary, which as we've seen may be just north of minimum wage. Students are also facing more obstacles than ever before as contemporary cultural and political events continue to expose academic and technology access gaps in education. Teachers who feel tired, ignored, and discouraged shouldn't be shunned for speaking up or for speaking their truth.

We are at a crossroads in education. A CNBC article reports that before the pandemic, researchers estimated that one out of six American teachers was likely to leave the profession. New survey data from the nonprofit RAND Corporation suggests that now one out of four teachers is considering quitting after this school year. According to the US Department of Education, almost all 50 states reported shortages for the 2020–2021 school year and the numbers aren't looking any better for the 2021–2022 school year.

Let's stop all the toxic positivity and look at education for where it is and have discussions about where it needs to go. This can't be solved with a dance or a vague, upbeat response on social media, but through true collaboration between all stakeholders, setting realistic expectations, and creating a school culture that ensures equity, excellence, and the eagerness to be the best it can be.

Chapter 27
Inclusion for All

I was the principal of two very different schools. The middle school was located in a lower-socioeconomic neighborhood that was populated mostly by Hispanic families. Most of our students were English language learners whose families emigrated to America for a better life. For some, they were working toward being the first person in their family to finish high school. Our goal was to have them be the first generation in their family to attend college.

The elementary school was in an upper-middle-class neighborhood. Most of the students were proficient English speakers and one or both parents had attended college.

The data coming out of these schools were drastically different. However, when you peel back the layers, some similarities could be seen.

The annual state test scores of the elementary school were insanely high. The school was routinely the highest performing in the district as well as in the top three in the county. It was easy to hide what was right in front of us. While the vast majority of our students were performing well, we had some students who were falling through the cracks. Those students were our English language learners, students with special needs, and students of color.

There are many ways to interpret data. Our school often celebrated how well our students were performing on state assessments.

There was a slight arrogance to it. Almost all of our students came into the school with one to two years of preschool as well as having been exposed to reading by educated parents from birth. It was easy to celebrate our success and paint a rosy picture of our school.

No one wanted to see the new picture I was going to paint.

As we discussed in Pillar One, Leadership, data doesn't serve a purpose unless you do something with it. Assessment dashboards and reports need to be filtered down to reveal progress or regression at the student group level. That is where things get interesting.

I extracted this data and prepared to share it at an all-staff meeting.

I began the presentation by sharing our overall assessment results. There were cheers and high fives around the room as I went through the eligible grades. Now don't get me wrong, I celebrated right along with them. I had an amazing group of teachers who worked hard each and every day.

The mood in the room changed when I presented the student group data. I quickly learned that this type of data had never been shared with teachers in the past. It was evident that our instructional practices were not reaching all students. Our most at-risk students needed additional support, structure, and scaffolding. Sadly, our school had a history of teaching everyone in the same way, using the same methods.

English Language Learners

It was common to hear around the school that English Language Development (ELD) is taught by the ELD teacher. At this school, ELD was a pull-out program, and students met with a different teacher individually or in a small group, depending on their needs. This also meant that they were missing valuable class time and instruction, falling further behind.

Pull-out programs also create a very public understanding of which students need additional support. The physical act of leaving one class for a special class can be seen through the eyes of ELD students as embarrassing. The other students in the classroom might also look down on these students since they are leaving to get extra help.

Creating opportunities for push-in programs can help to alleviate this stigma; also, providing ELD instruction to all students is just good teaching. ELD instruction can be categorized into five main areas.

Language Acquisition: ELD instruction is based on the principles of language acquisition. Students are taught English language skills, such as listening, speaking, reading, and writing, in a way that is similar to how they acquired their first language.

Scaffolded Instruction: ELD instruction is scaffolded, meaning it provides support for learners at different levels of proficiency. Teachers use a variety of techniques, such as modeling, visual aids, and interactive activities to help students understand and use English.

Language Development: ELD instruction focuses on language development. Students are taught academic language and vocabulary specific to different subject areas. The goal is for students to be able to communicate effectively in academic settings.

Cultural Understanding: ELD instruction also includes teaching students about the cultural aspects of English-speaking countries. This includes social norms, customs, and traditions that are different from their own culture.

Integration with Content Instruction: ELD instruction is integrated with content instruction, meaning that students learn English while also learning content from other subject areas. This helps students make connections between language and content, and reinforces their learning.

If you read through these five ELD areas and are thinking that they just seem like good teaching strategies for all students, you would be right. Infusing ELD strategies for all students helps to create a strong instructional program and a more inclusive environment for all students.

Principals play a crucial role in supporting English language learners within their schools. By implementing various strategies, principals can create an inclusive and supportive environment that fosters the academic and linguistic growth of ELLs.

First, principals can ensure that teachers receive ongoing professional development on effective instructional strategies for ELLs. This includes training on language acquisition, differentiated instruction, and culturally responsive teaching. By equipping teachers with the necessary tools and knowledge, principals empower them to provide high-quality instruction that meets the unique needs of ELLs.

One of the most important aspects of principals supporting English language learners is to allocate resources to support language development. This includes providing instructional materials, technology, and multilingual resources. Principals can also allocate funds and personnel to offer targeted support services, such as English as a Second Language (ESL) classes or bilingual aides. By prioritizing these resources, principals demonstrate their commitment to providing equitable educational opportunities for ELLs.

Fostering family engagement to support ELLs' academic success can help the whole family feel welcomed and supported. Families can encourage teachers to establish regular communication with families, provide translated materials, and organize events that celebrate diverse cultures. By involving families in their children's education, principals build a strong support network that promotes positive academic outcomes for English language learners.

Depending on the location, some principals will play a critical role in supporting students who have recently immigrated to the country and are adjusting to a new school and culture. Principals need to ensure that newcomers feel comfortable from the moment they enter the school. This can involve assigning a specifically chosen staff member or peer buddy to guide them through the initial orientation process. Ideally, this staff member or buddy student will speak the home language of the new student. Principals can also facilitate orientations that provide information about the school's resources, procedures, and support systems available to newcomers in their home language. By creating a welcoming, inclusive, and informative environment, principals help students who are new to the country navigate the challenges of their new school setting.

It is vital that principals promote culturally responsive practices within the school community to acknowledge and value the diverse backgrounds of newcomers. This includes encouraging teachers to incorporate culturally relevant materials and instructional strategies that reflect the experiences and perspectives of the students. Principals can also organize cultural events, celebrations, or assemblies that allow newcomers to share their cultures with the wider school community. By embracing and celebrating diversity, principals create an inclusive environment where newcomers feel accepted and valued.

Principals can ensure that effective communication channels are in place to engage with families of newcomers. This includes providing language support services, such as translated materials or interpreters, to overcome language barriers. Principals can also establish regular communication channels, such as newsletters, emails, or online platforms, to keep families informed about school events, academic progress, and available resources. By facilitating clear and accessible communication, principals empower families to actively participate in their child's education.

Setting up collaborative partnerships between the school and community organizations that provide support to families can be one of the most important elements in ensuring that the family is being taken care of properly. This can involve connecting families with local resources, such as social services, health-care providers, or language learning programs. Principals can also organize workshops or information sessions on topics such as navigating the education system, supporting homework, or promoting cultural understanding. By fostering these partnerships, principals expand the support network available to new families and help address their unique needs beyond the school setting.

Students with Special Needs

The same ideas utilized for English language learners and their families can be applied to students with special needs, with some variables.

Depending on the specialized needs of the student, there will be cases where a child should be in a self-contained classroom in order to receive the best education possible. However, schools should define times and learning opportunities for students to be with their grade-level peers. There could be multiple opportunities for push-in instruction so that students can experience the general classroom setting. General classroom teachers should also be well versed in the child's IEP so that they can provide the necessary support needed.

Classroom teachers can use specialized instructional strategies and materials to help students with special needs learn and access the curriculum. This can be accomplished in the general classroom setting as well as the self-contained classroom. In some cases, students can be helped by providing them assistive technology. This can include devices such as computer programs, tablets, speech-to-text software, manipulatives, and hearing aids. These devices can help a student be more self-sufficient in the classroom as well as give them the ability to fully participate in discussions.

IEP meetings are some of the most important facets of an educator's job. Ensuring that appropriate placement and services are being provided for some of our most at-risk students should always be a top priority. It is vital that these meetings be productive, collaborative, and student focused. Sadly, too often such meetings get derailed by emotions, politics, and a fundamental difference of beliefs.

Parents do not want to be surprised during an IEP meeting, especially in front of the entire IEP team. Results of assessments should be discussed with parents before the meeting takes place. The special education teacher, support provider, and/or school psychologist should call or meet with the family to discuss results or qualifications ahead of time so that they can digest the information before the meeting, and think of questions to ask without being rushed.

I have worked with parents from all backgrounds. There is a common thread that runs through all of them – they want the very best for their child. Parents need to be an integral part of the conversation. Make sure they understand everything that is being said by using layman's terms instead of complicated education terms or acronyms. You don't want to tell a parent that their RSP child scored in the Standard Not Met category, or a level 4, of the ELA portion of the CAASPP and that you are recommending them for more MTSS/RTI.

I have a firm belief that nothing productive happens in meetings after an hour has passed. Having a clear time frame will help the team move the meeting along and keep sidebar conversations to a minimum, so that the real energy can be spent focused on the child.

Parents want to see tangible evidence of their child's progress or regression. Bringing in work samples, assessments, and behavior trackers will give parents an opportunity to see concrete examples of their child's efforts. These samples of work and behavior bring real data to the table. Without that, an IEP team is just speaking in opinions and theories.

Smile. Yes, smile. Always remember that you are meeting with a parent who wants the best for their child and that they are possibly anxious about what the future holds for their family. For initial assessment IEP meetings, parents are in unfamiliar waters. Put them at ease. Even if you don't agree, always remember to smile, be pleasant, and listen to their concerns. Discourse doesn't always have to be unpleasant.

Principals play a crucial role in creating an inclusive environment for students with special needs. School leaders must promote a culture of acceptance and understanding within the school community by educating students, teachers, and staff about disabilities and special needs. This can involve organizing awareness campaigns, workshops, or assemblies that address misconceptions and promote empathy and respect for students with special needs.

All teachers and staff must receive ongoing professional development on inclusive practices and strategies for supporting students with special needs. Too often, these professional development sessions are designed for just teachers who work exclusively with students with special needs. This includes training on differentiation, Universal Design for Learning (UDL), and effective instructional techniques. By equipping all educators on campus with the necessary knowledge and skills, principals create an inclusive learning environment where students with special needs can thrive.

When was the last time your school was assessed for ADA compliance? If you don't know, you are not alone. Principals must ensure that the physical environment of the school is accessible and accommodating for students with special needs. This may involve making modifications such as putting in wheelchair ramps, widening doorways, creating accessible restrooms, or designating specialized sensory spaces. Principals can also collaborate with teachers and specialists to create sensory-friendly classrooms and implement visual supports, assistive technology, and adaptive equipment to meet the diverse needs of students. This will help special needs students when they are in the general education setting.

Celebrating the diversity and accomplishments of students with special needs within the school community is a great way to promote an inclusive culture. This can involve highlighting the achievements of students with special needs, showcasing their talents, and organizing inclusive events that encourage the participation and appreciation of all students. By recognizing and valuing the contributions of students with special needs, principals promote a sense of belonging and boost their self-esteem.

Race

Race was the most difficult area to address. I wanted to ensure that I didn't point any fingers at anyone with any assumptions. The meeting was already tense. I didn't want it to get away from me. This is where the notion of being clinical, not critical, comes back into play.

I let the data speak for itself and asked teachers what their thoughts were on it.

Data doesn't lie. You could look at our assessment data on the charts and graphs, broken down by subgroups, and not see that this was a problem. The room was silent for what seemed like an eternity.

Then they spoke up.

And owned it.

The majority of the students at the school were white; however, we did have students who were African American, Hispanic, and Asian. In order to strengthen the culture of our school, we had to ensure that we were honoring the rich experiences and backgrounds of our students.

Teachers can celebrate the diversity of their students by displaying posters and other materials that represent different cultures and ethnicities. They can also incorporate books and other materials that reflect the experiences of students from diverse backgrounds. This can go down to the more granular level by providing students with problems to work through that include names and experiences from a wide range of cultures.

Teachers need to value all students' experiences by encouraging them to share their cultures and experiences with their classmates. This can be done through classroom discussions, group activities, and presentations. Teachers can also use cultural events, literature, and other resources to help students learn about different perspectives and backgrounds.

Sometimes, teachers will need to address negative behaviors and language that may be hurtful or discriminatory by encouraging positive behaviors that promote acceptance and respect. This can be achieved by having inclusion activities be a natural part of daily instruction.

Building strong relationships is the key to creating a welcoming and inclusive school culture. Administrators and teachers can build relationships with students and families from different cultures by communicating regularly, seeking their input, and attending cultural events and celebrations. Furthermore, being open to learning about different cultures and traditions by attending workshops, conferences, and other professional development opportunities can show families that the school cares about connecting and celebrating with everyone.

When addressing race at your school, do yourself a favor and take a walk into the school library. Take a look around. What do you see?

Do you see different races and cultures represented in posters on the walls?

Do the featured books at all grade levels have protagonists from different cultures?

Are different perspectives celebrated in the library collection?

The school library is an important spot in a school. Not only is it a place where all students go throughout the day, but it is often the room that is used for larger parent meetings. When parents walk into your school's library, do they see posters, books, and materials that represent their culture? If they don't, they might feel like an outsider. If they feel that way, it is a good bet that their child does, too.

Inclusion ideals are important for staff members as well. It is easy for teachers to create silos for themselves and others. Some do this subconsciously while others purposefully retreat to their own islands so that they don't have to change their teaching practices or to face the fact that their methods aren't working.

The research is very clear on teacher collaboration: it works. A recent study by Ronfeldt, Farmer, McQueen, and Grissom (2015) surveyed over 9,000 teachers on the subject of teacher collaboration. Over 90% of the teachers surveyed indicated that collaboration was beneficial to both teachers and their students. At every school, however, there are teachers who are reluctant to collaborate with their colleagues.

Teachers have enough on their plate. It is important that they don't feel that collaboration time is just another meeting they must attend with no actionable outcomes. Each collaborative team should sit down and outline the purpose and expected outcomes of their time together. This creates a sense of responsibility and direction. It also encourages teachers to come to meetings prepared to share recent data, work samples, and questions. It also helps to prevent collaboration time from being hijacked and turned into a complaint session.

Creating opportunities for teachers to collaborate during the school day will help them engage. Some teachers have trouble being fully engaged at a 7:15 a.m. or 4:00 p.m. team meeting. Having collaboration time during the school day honors their contract and maximizes their potential to collaborate without the distractions of being tired or having to leave to pick up their own children or make appointments. Scheduling collaboration during the day also allows administrators to mandate attendance if necessary.

Some reluctant collaborators are afraid to let their guard down to their colleagues. It is important to validate these feelings and put them at ease. Having a one-on-one conversation outside of the meeting will give these teachers an opportunity to express their concerns and fears in a safe and confidential environment. Sometimes, being reluctant and being withdrawn from a group is a defense mechanism so that these teachers don't feel inadequate or antiquated.

In some cases, schools want to have collaborative teams up and running and looking at data in record time. Before teams dive into that work, they need to be provided the time and space to come together and define themselves. Tuckman (1965) gives us five distinct stages of team development: Forming, Storming, Norming, Performing, and Adjourning. Once teams are formed, administration needs to allow them to storm in order to formulate their identity. The storming process allows for teachers to discuss norms, intentions, best practices, and communication protocols. Once this is allowed to occur, teams can begin to norm themselves based on the outcomes of the storming process. Without the storming process to occur, team members will still be battling for position and air time leading to poorly developed norms.

Teachers will feel more engaged if they feel they have a purpose or a role in a meeting. One way to do this is to ensure that reluctant teachers have a specific role or job in their collaborative team meeting. Jobs could be anything from note taker to time keeper, facilitator to administration liaison. These roles are important not only for the operation of the collaborative team, but also for the self-esteem and motivation of a reluctant collaborator.

What Now?

Changing the culture of a school is hard work. It is not something that can be accomplished in a few days, weeks, or even months – but it can be done. Changing your school's culture starts with observing. Here is how to get started:

1. Walk the halls and note what you see. Is student work present? Do posters and imagery reflect the student body, the teachers, or both?
2. Spend some time in the library. Whenever I needed a quiet place to work, I went into the library. I also had an alternative motive. I wanted to see what books were available for our students. The question here is the same: Do the books reflect the student body?
3. Take a look at the composition of the committees at the school site. Are all stakeholders represented? Is there an equitable distribution of race, ethnicity, gender, and backgrounds?

Chapter 28
Creating a Safe Environment

There are many aspects to creating a safe school environment for students and teachers alike. Principals need to consider not just the physical safety of students and teachers, but also the emotional safety of students in our complex, technology-driven world.

It is unfortunate that schools need to spend a considerable amount of time ensuring the physical safety of students and staff. It is a sad sign of the times that will be with us for a very long time. Today's parents no longer have the same peace of mind they had just a few decades ago, that they're sending their children to a safe place when they wave good-bye in the morning. Schools today must plan for the unthinkable and prepare their teachers, staff, and students to survive by escaping an intruder intent on creating as many casualties as possible. I never liked sending home the email to parents letting them know that we were having an active shooter drill. However, it is a necessary aspect of our work as school leaders and there is a right way and a wrong way to conduct these drills.

Intruder drills can be scary for everyone involved. It's therefore vital that schools clearly communicate with teachers, parents, students, school neighbors, and local law enforcement the purpose and scope of the drill. The last thing anyone wants is to create an atmosphere of fear that can traumatize students, teachers, staff, and parents. As such, this type of drill should never be conducted without an effort to interface with all stakeholders beforehand. You also do not want surprised and scared students texting their parents that they are sheltering in place, not knowing that it is only a drill.

School leaders should not attempt to plan and conduct this type of drill on their own. It is vital that principals partner with local law enforcement to educate the staff on current safety protocols. New best practices are always being created and it is essential that educators understand the latest research and techniques. It's also important to have first responders on-site to assist with the drill to provide immediate and expert feedback as well as suggestions for improvement. The first responders present at the drill will likely be the same ones if an active shooter does come onto campus. By attending the drill, first responders will learn the layout of the school, including access points, hiding spots, and key personnel. I was amazed at how much feedback I received from my drill that I never would have considered.

There are dozens of tools available that can be wedged into doors and prevent them from opening. However, most first responders do not like these as they end up doing more harm by preventing emergency personnel from entering the room if needed. While these tools do a good job of keeping the door in place, they can also prevent students and staff from easily opening doors from the inside if they need to evacuate a room. Furthermore, most classrooms have windows that can be broken to gain entry, leaving students and staff exposed and trapped.

I once worked with a teacher who did not have their students shelter in place behind chairs and desks at all. Instead, she used a door tie to secure the door shut. Unfortunately, right next to the door were about 20 feet of windows that could be easily kicked in and broken so that an intruder could gain access to the classroom.

First responders recommend students and staff create door barricades made of desks, cabinets, chairs, and tables. They also recommend building a second internal barricade for students and staff to hide behind in case the door barricade is breached. Desk and tables should be overturned in the corner of the room that is the least visible from the doorway. Students and staff should remain behind this barricade and out of sight from the intruder. Active shooter profile research from the Department of Homeland Security tells us that if the intruder can't easily see a victim, they will move on to the next location.

As stated, it's important for schools to communicate with all stakeholders that an active intruder drill will be taking place; however, schools should not publish the actual time of the drill. In the vast majority of school shootings, the shooter is connected to the school in some way. Law enforcement recommends not providing detailed day and time information to the general public, as this might give the individual the opportunity to see the safety procedures in action and then adjust their plan to evade capture or inflict more harm.

One study from the Department of Homeland Security breaks down the affiliation of an intruder to the school. It indicates that over 70% of school shooters have a direct affiliation to the school with the vast majority being current students. The rest of this group is composed of former students, parents of current students, and individuals who have approval to be on campus for sporting events.

This means that the majority of school shooters have complete and total access to school grounds, buildings, and classrooms. These individuals are able to walk past any and all physical security measures, including fencing, school resources officers, and surveillance cameras. Still, school districts spend hundreds of thousands of dollars on new security fencing and HD cameras in an effort to deter violence. According to the *Washington Post*, school shootings have fueled a school security industry worth $2.7 billion (Cox & Rich, 2018).

Such precautionary measures would only be beneficial if the shooter does not have an affiliation with the school.

- Sandy Hook Elementary School had security fences in place. The shooter was the son of a substitute teacher. Twenty children and six staff members were killed.

- Stoneman Douglas High School employed an SRO. The shooter, a former student at SDHS, was able to enter the school building after the outer doors were unlocked for dismissal. Fourteen students and three teachers were killed.
- Sante Fe High School employed two SROs. The shooter was a current student. Nine students and one teacher died.
- Saugus High School had security fences and cameras throughout the campus. The shooter was a current student. Two students died in the attack.
- Robb Elementary School had self-locking doors that did not work properly. Nineteen children and two staff members were killed.

The results of these shootings are tragic. In the school year 2012–2022, 225 children left for school in the morning and never made it home. This problem simply cannot be stopped by installing fences and security cameras.

The solution requires a more proactive and comprehensive approach.

According to the US Department of Health and Human Services, one in five children experiences a mental health problem during their school years. Examples of mental health problems include stress, anxiety, bullying, family problems, depression, learning disabilities, as well as alcohol and substance abuse. Serious mental health problems, such as self-injurious behaviors and suicide, are on the rise, particularly among youth. Unfortunately, up to 60% of students do not receive the mental health treatment they need due to social stigma and lack of access to services. Of those who do get help, nearly two-thirds do so only in school.

The Child Mind Institute (2015) reports that half of all mental illness occurs before the age of 14, with 75% by the age of 24. These statistics highlight the need for schools to be able to address mental health concerns early on and with fidelity, an approach that focuses on early intervention strategies rather than last-minute crisis response. It's imperative that these at-risk students be given the support they need before they engage in dangerous and violent behavior.

Unfortunately, the mental health services that are present in school exist mostly at the high school level. These programs are constantly acting in a crisis mode as many of the teenagers that these programs serve have already been exposed to some level of trauma in the past. It is vital to provide mental health services for students earlier in life. A 2018 study from the Center for Health and Health Care in Schools reports that "students who receive positive behavioral health interventions see improvements on a range of behaviors related to academic achievement, beyond letter grades or test scores" (Walker, 2018).

Building fences and installing cameras will not provide these struggling students the support they need. School systems need to invest more time and resources to the mental health and well-being of all their students. Principals need to ensure that there are sufficient counselors and other mental health providers on campus to support students in nonacademic areas. Furthermore, schools should employ a social-emotional learning platform to immerse students in self-reflection and self-awareness.

According to Media Smarts (n.d.), 23% of students reported that they've said or done something cruel to another person online and 27% reported that they've experienced the same from someone else. With the increased use of collaboration tools and social media, children can be bullied 24 hours a day, 7 days a week.

School leaders, parents, and students need to address this issue head-on as students should no longer be fearful of being bullied both at school or online when they are at home.

Students need to report cyberbullying to an adult. Unfortunately, according to the National Crime Prevention Council (n.d.), only 1 in 10 children will report cyberbullying to a trusted adult or parent. An important step is to make reporting this type of abuse easier and less stigmatizing.

Sadly, the phrase "snitches get stitches" is still used today.

In order to circumvent this problem, schools could create anonymous ways for students to report bullying of others or of themselves. There are a variety of online tools that can support schools in this capacity.

Bullies engage in harmful behavior because they want to elicit a response from their victim. By not engaging, the potential victim exercises their power and can end the bullying before it ever gains traction. Responding to the bully will almost always make the bullying worse and last longer. The more students who understand this, the better.

School systems need to hold cyberbullies accountable for their actions. Schools should seriously consider including cyberbullying into their disciplinary matrix to ensure that all stakeholders are aware of its definition and consequences. It is also vital that we teach children to stand up and report bullying when they see it. Some students have a very difficult time sharing emotions with adults, so encouraging a culture of collective accountability will make it easier for so many children.

Children need to understand that posting hurtful comments online about someone hurts as much if not more than if the comments were to their faces. Once posted, online comments can be seen by anyone who has access to the social media account or webpage. They must understand that they are posting about a real person who will be reading what was said. They are not simply typing words into a computer or a phone.

These ideas need to be instilled in our students. Having a robust digital citizenship program is essential for all schools. While many schools are hyper-focused on academic curriculum, I would agree that this type of curriculum is just as important.

What Now?

Student safety has sadly become a major talking point around the world in recent years. Parents need to feel confident that their children will be safe at school during the day and that they will come home in the afternoon. The reasons for these school safety concerns are complex and need to be addressed by the administration. Here's how to get started:

1. Conduct a facilities check of the campus. This should be completed monthly. Make sure all doors lock as they are supposed to and ingress and egress points are secured. Report any issues to district maintenance immediately.
2. Create a physical anonymous counselor's box or an online form for students to complete to get help. Many students will not publicly address their depression, anxiety, or anger. Having multiple ways for students to get help on campus is a good start.
3. Declare the school a no-bullying zone. Bullying leads to destructive behaviors on both ends of the spectrum. Students who bully others need to be disciplined and their behavior addressed with their parents. Too many schools let these behaviors slide. Similar to the counselor's box, creating an online tip form for reporting bullying will help students feel more confident about reporting.

Chapter 29

Sharing Your Own Story

I t goes without saying that, for better or for worse, social media has transformed communication. Pictures, videos, and comments can be easily posted and sent to followers in an instant. Social media gives school leaders another opportunity to share activities, programs, and student learning with the greater community and the world at large.

Unfortunately, schools continue to lag in this area, with educators still reluctant to use social media.

Teachers spend their entire day working with students. They engage them in thoughtful, exciting, and innovative projects, conversations, and ideas. As a parent, I would love to see and hear more of these interactions. Working parents who do not have the flexibility to volunteer on a regular basis in their child's classroom miss out on experiencing day-to-day interactions. Principals can take pictures of classrooms, activities, and the inner workings of a school throughout the day, giving followers a glimpse into a day at the school. This will give them a window into that world from anywhere in the world.

Give yourself a half hour to go exploring. Trust me, you'll be hooked.

Creating a strong social media presence is not just for the adults on campus; however, having students on social media can strike fear into even the most progressive educator. Nevertheless, we all know that most students are already engaging in social media in some capacity. It is vital that we teach them to be responsible while they are online and with what they post. We need to help students develop their voice and at the same time ensure they do not leave a digital footprint that will haunt them for years to come.

Some ideas for students to get involved in creating the story for a school is to post about activities, sports, and happenings at the school using a school hashtag. I have been interested in the notion of school branding for some time now. With parents having more options in their child's education than ever before, I believe that schools need to do a better job in "selling" the mission and vision of their school to the public and in sharing celebrations of student learning. Students are the best school ambassadors out there. Let them share their story.

Sharing pictures, videos, and comments helps bridge the knowledge gap for parents. As parents become increasingly informed, they will be inclined to step forward to volunteer and become active on vital school committees, such as School Site Council, PTA, and ELAC.

What Now?

This is the fun part! Social media can be a great outlet for positivity, connection, and the sharing of best practices. Not sure where to get started? Here are some ideas:

1. Start taking pictures. Lots of pictures. The purpose of the social media accounts is to share the day-to-day happenings at the school with parents, community members, and stakeholders. Don't be shy in publicizing the great things that are happening at your site.

2. Send out social media consent forms to all students at the beginning of the year. Make sure you have permission up front to share the images of your students.

3. Get others involved in posting content. The principal should not be the sole contributor to a social media account. Engage lead teachers, your office manager, and other administrators in posting too in order to create a vivid story to share with your community.

Chapter 30

Creating a Collaborative Culture from the Ground Up

The best schools are those where school leaders, teachers, staff members, parents, and community members are on the same page. This starts with creating a collective vision statement.

A school's vision statement is often overlooked, hidden, or inexplicably nonexistent. It can be found on most schools' websites, hidden among bell schedules, lunch options, teacher websites, and PTA pages. Teachers and administrators often don't know what is written in their school's vision statement. Parents don't either. Students . . . well, you get the picture.

What about your school? Would you be able to recite or discuss your school's vision statement without it in front of you?

Shouldn't we all know the ideological foundation of the institution where we send our children or work at each and every day?

A school's vision statement should be dynamic, specific, and forward thinking. Statements should no longer make simple, generic claims like:

1. We are preparing students for the future.
2. We believe all students can learn.
3. Together, we are making our community strong.

Remember, a vision statement is like a roadmap. It tells a story of where you are going and how you are going to get there.

Many teachers and administrators inherit generic school visions when they get hired. Individuals who are no longer connected with the school created these forgettable statements decades ago. These statements were also created when educational practices, expectations, and tools were different. Do yourself and your school community a favor and start over.

The best statements are created by a diverse group of stakeholders including teachers, administrators, parents, community members, and students. Make sure they are all involved in creating the school's vision statement. This way, buy-in from these groups will be easier to gain.

Too many school vision statements are stale, lifeless creations that don't mean anything in the real world. They only exist in the vacuum of the page, not in the collective consciousness of the school. When someone steps onto your campus they should be able to see, hear, and feel the vision in action. This notion takes place at all levels of the school from the front office to the cafeteria, to classrooms, hallways, and playgrounds.

Men and women in sales perfect their elevator pitch every day. Pretend you are riding up an elevator with another person. As the doors are closing, they ask you to explain what makes your school special or different from others. You have until the elevator stops at their floor to answer them – about 30 seconds. Could you do it? Could your staff do it? Parents? Students?

Try it.

Have your teachers try it.

A school's vision statement needs to be publicized and should be front and center in every communication. Give it a central location on the school's website. It should be a part of the header of paper communications and included in the email signatures of staff members. Furthermore, the school's vision should be consulted when making program, budget, and personnel decisions. You will want the decision-making process and outcomes to match the collectively created school vision that makes the school unique.

Trust is the foundation on which productive teams are built. Remember, as Seth Godin said, earn trust, earn trust, earn trust. Then you can worry about the rest.

Closed doors leave a lot to the imagination. The principal's door should be open as much as possible. When parents come into the office when picking up their child early or signing in to volunteer, they'll be able to see you. A quick hello can go a long way in building trust and respect.

Some principals make changes without consulting staff members, teachers, or students. These changes are made centrally and without input from those who will be required to make the changes. Strong school leaders listen to their leadership team, parents, and students when it comes to either making changes or keeping things the same.

A school is no place for smoke and mirrors. Taking on a cold war approach to communication and information gathering is not necessary. Decisions should never be made in a back room without representation from different stakeholder groups. Leaders build up social capital in their team, not create rubber-stamp delegations.

Principals must not only talk the talk, but walk the walk. This is meant literally and figuratively. Get out of the office. Walk around, visit classrooms, work the parking lot, talk to parents. Do not be the invisible principal. Invisible principals spend their days in their office with the door closed sending emails. Get out of the office. Take a walk.

Principals need to be student-centered. They do not take sides other than doing what is in the best interest of the students. While that might make a principal unpopular from time to time, it will also make them respected. You can't have trust without respect. Being student-centered keeps the focus on the purpose of schools – to educate children.

Great schools and districts all have one thing in common: great organizational culture. Dedicated teachers and a research-based curriculum isn't enough to make a school great. Culture is everything. Management guru Peter Drucker wrote, "Culture eats strategy for lunch." He was right. A poor organizational culture will send these amazing teachers straight into the arms of another school or district.

Teachers and principals need to be focused on one thing: their students. Too often, their focus is shifted from maximizing student achievement to compliance issues, paperwork, or other aspects that are not important or urgent. However, they will get email after email and memo after memo reminding them to complete these tasks that will have no bearing on student achievement. Let them keep their focus on students. Trust that they know what their students need. After all, they are with them all day long.

We all know that educators have a smaller chance of having cosmetic maintenance orders processed than walking on the moon. However, never underestimate the impact that small changes can make. Consider smaller improvements that will make a big impact such as new paint on playground benches, planter barrels in front of every classroom, new decor in the staff room, new posters for every room, and so on. Classrooms can go decades without being painted. If you are lucky enough to be able to do it, go for it. I have never seen teachers so happy before or since the day they were surprised by fresh paint in their classrooms.

Want to brighten up everyone's day? Try this: Once a month, have your student council dress up a book cart with a tablecloth, flowers in a vase, fresh coffee, and pastries. Have them go from classroom to classroom treating teachers. For less than 40 bucks, you will make everyone's morning. You can always make hot chocolate or tea for non-coffee drinkers!

No one likes to have decisions dictated from the top down. Teachers and principals must be trusted to make decisions for the students they work with. These decisions need to come from within, not from downtown. As I stated earlier, teachers and principals are the ones with their students all day long.

Notice how the media always focuses on the negatives? There always seems to be a story on corrupt administration, money siphoning, abuse scandals . . .

We need to interject some positive stories into our community's collective consciousness. While we can't always control what the local paper or news stations report, we can control what we put out. It is essential that educators utilize social media and websites to share daily successes with their community. Create Twitter and Facebook accounts to share the hard work of educators each and every day. Educators are happier when they are receiving praise for their hard work.

What Now?

A collaborative culture comes from careful decision making. This step must be conducted in collaboration with stakeholders across the school community. Here is how to get started:

1. Find out when the mission statement for the school was written. Then, find out how many staff members who are still working at the school were present at that time. That will tell you if it is time for a new mission statement.
2. Create a teacher coffee delivery calendar. The coffee cart mentioned in this chapter is a hit in many schools across the country. But as mentioned many times before, if it is not on your calendar, it will be easy to forget.
3. Be visible from the start. Be outside in the hallways, classrooms, and parking lot more than inside your office. Be seen. Be noticeable. Be present.

Tales from the
Principal's Desk

Close your eyes and think of an elementary school.
What do you see? What do you hear?
When most of us think about an elementary school setting, we think of young children running around the playground, engaged in art projects, learning the building blocks of reading, writing, and math, participating in cultural events, going to music class, and waiting in line for the hot lunch of the day. It's noisy, active, but controlled and defined by routines.

When I began my tenure at my elementary school, I walked into a school that was all business. The school was heavy in academics. Some of the teachers defined themselves as strict and gave a ton of homework because they had "high expectations." As the year got off the ground, I watched, listened, and experienced the school's culture firsthand. The teachers at the school were very dedicated, knowledgeable on academic content, and strong classroom managers. But something was missing.

Fun.

This school felt more like a high-pressure college preparatory school than an elementary school. August and September came and went and I prepared myself to experience October and my first Halloween as an elementary school principal. Coming from the middle school level, I was excited to be a part of this event at the elementary level as all middle school educators know that Halloween at the middle school level can get a little too interesting with the costumes.

Then, I learned the truth.

My school didn't do Halloween.

It didn't do Halloween, not because of a religious or cultural reason, but because some teachers believed that it was too much of a distraction in the learning process. They didn't want to deal with students in their costumes or with students who were "out of control" and "overly excitable" on that day.

Um . . . it's Halloween. They're supposed to be excited. I have fond memories of dressing up and going to school in my costume, seeing what my friends picked for their costumes, and enjoying a day of games and fun.

At the time, my school had been open for 35 years. Halloween had never been something that teachers or students celebrated. I was disappointed. Not just for the students, but for myself as well. I was looking forward to dressing up!

One afternoon, a second-grade teacher came into my office. She wanted to talk about Halloween. He explained that while it seemed that the staff as a whole didn't want to celebrate Halloween, it was really just a handful of the more veteran teachers who always shut down the possibility of having students dress up. Every year, parents asked me when the school would allow students to dress up in costumes for Halloween.

I thought about it and decided to talk to some of the teachers who might feel the same way. She was right. Most of the teachers I spoke to were in favor of bringing Halloween to the school. The word was out that I was asking about this issue. I had a few unhappy teachers storm into my office telling me that I was going against the culture and history of the school. I told them that I believed in having everyone's voice be a part of the conversation and that this is a topic that we would be discussing at our next meeting. If the majority of the staff didn't want students to dress up for Halloween, then everything would stay status quo, because I valued the opinion of everyone.

Our staff meetings were on Wednesdays. I spent Monday and Tuesday preparing myself for this potentially contentious conversation. The second-grade teacher who started this off gave me her son's football helmet to use as a prop to lighten the mood a bit.

I went into the meeting with butterflies in my stomach. I knew that this conversation would be emotional. I brought up the elephant in the room right away. I wanted everyone to be a part of the conversation and ensured that everyone who wanted to speak had the opportunity to address their peers.

The second-grade teacher spoke up as well as several of the veteran teachers who opposed bringing Halloween to the school. You could feel the tension in the room as well as the subtle feeling of intimidation from some of the veteran staff.

Keep in mind, the entire time I was wearing the football helmet.

After everyone had the opportunity to address their peers, I told the staff that we would put it to a vote. The teachers who did not want to change quickly requested that we conduct the vote out in the open.

I said no.

I saw what they were doing. I would not let any teachers feel intimidated or reluctant to express their viewpoint. I gave everyone a slip of paper and told them to write YES or NO. Once they had written their response, I told them to crumble the paper into a ball and throw it at me. Yes, I was still wearing the helmet. I told everyone that once they threw the paper at me, they had to let go of any frustration and accept the outcome of the vote.

I never could have imagined how many elementary school teachers could have had careers as pitchers in the MLB!

I counted the votes in front of everyone and announced the results.

18 to 4 in favor of Halloween.

I was shocked at how lopsided the vote was.

Democracy was alive and well at this elementary school. While there were a few teachers who were initially upset at the outcome of the vote, they did not create any roadblocks moving forward since they saw that the decision was made in a collaborative environment. Everyone was heard. Everyone was valued.

My second-grade teacher was beyond happy. So were most of the other teachers.

Parents came up to me in the parking lot at arrival and school dismissal excited about the change as well as wanting to confirm that it was real.

That Halloween, for the first time in the school's history, kids dressed up in costumes, participated in Halloween-themed games, and experienced a rite of passage that many of us enjoyed as kids.

Now I'm not going to lie, the next day was rough.

But it was worth it.

Questions to Ask Yourself

- What values and beliefs underpin our school's culture? Reflect on your school's core values, beliefs, and guiding principles and consider whether these values are explicitly communicated and consistently modeled by school leaders, teachers, and staff. Assess whether the school's culture promotes inclusivity, respect, collaboration, and a sense of belonging for all members of the school community.
- How are we fostering a positive and supportive school climate? Reflect on the overall climate and atmosphere within the school. Consider whether it is conducive to a positive learning environment and the well-being of students, teachers, and staff. Assess whether there are systems in place to address issues such as bullying, harassment, and conflict resolution. Reflect on how well the school promotes social-emotional learning, fosters positive relationships, and supports the mental health and emotional well-being of all members of the school community.
- How are we promoting a culture of continuous improvement and professional growth? Reflect on your school's approach and consider whether there is a culture of ongoing professional

growth for teachers and staff. Assess whether there are structures in place, such as coaching, mentoring, and collaborative learning communities, to support professional development and the sharing of best practices. Reflect on how well the school encourages innovation, embraces change, and provides opportunities for all stakeholders to contribute to the improvement of the school's culture and practices.

Conclusion

The job of a new principal is a difficult one. There is a reason why most educators never get into administration. There is also a reason why most principals only last three years at their school site. The hours are long, the stress is high, everything is your fault, no one calls or emails to tell you about something good, but everyone calls or emails with their complaints and grievances. Nonetheless, the decade that I spent at the principal's desk was extremely rewarding, fulfilling, and humbling.

When I was in high school, I got good grades, but wasn't particularly academic. I also never truly liked school. In college, I majored in music so that I could fulfill my dreams of rock stardom. I started substitute teaching to pay the rent and to have a job that allowed me to practice and perform at night. When I became a full-time teacher, I never imagined that I would be the principal of not just one, but two schools. And not just two schools, but two award-winning schools that earned accolades for instruction, programming, and innovation.

There will be ups and downs in your journey. There will be times when you don't want to get out of bed in the morning, and there will be times when you didn't think you could be prouder of your school community. While the instant gratification of being a teacher and seeing that lightbulb go off is no longer there, you get to experience the afterglow of that realization from students across your school.

As you begin your leadership journey, ask yourself the following questions that are tied to the five pillars to guide your decision-making to ensure you are effectively meeting the needs of your school community from the beginning. Ask yourself these questions when you feel lost and need to recalibrate. It is easy to lose your way in this difficult and unpredictable job. However, use the answers to these questions as your guiding compass. Your North Star.

1. What is my leadership philosophy and vision for the school? Reflect on your core beliefs and values as an educational leader. Collaborate on your vision for the school with stakeholder groups and establish clear goals that align with the values and the needs of the students, teachers, and community.

2. How can I build positive relationships with staff, students, and parents? Recognize the importance of building strong relationships and fostering a positive school culture. Consider strategies to engage and collaborate with staff, establish rapport with students, and actively involve parents and families in the educational process. Think about ways to be visible to all stakeholders.

3. What are the strengths and areas for improvement within the school? Conduct a comprehensive assessment of the school's strengths and weaknesses in regard to academic achievement, cultural inclusion, and overall reputation. Identify areas for improvement and develop plans to address them. Recognize and leverage the strengths to promote positive change and enhance student outcomes.

4. How can I support and develop the teachers and staff? Acknowledge the critical role of teachers and staff in the success of the

school. Teachers and staff members will always be the biggest catalyst of change. Consider ways to support their professional growth through targeted professional development, coaching, and mentoring. Create a culture of collaboration, innovation, and continuous learning. That way, you will not only retain great teachers, but attract new ones as well.

5. How can I ensure an inclusive and equitable learning environment? Commit to creating an inclusive and equitable school where every student feels valued, supported, and an important part of the school community. Reflect on strategies to address diversity, equity, and inclusion. Evaluate policies, practices, and resources to promote equal opportunities and meet the needs of all students.

6. How can I effectively communicate and engage with all stakeholders? Recognize the importance of effective communication and engagement with all stakeholders, including staff, students, parents, and the community. Consider different modes of communication, such as regular newsletters, email, meetings, and social media, to ensure transparency, collaboration, and a sense of shared responsibility.

7. How can I foster a safe and supportive learning environment? Prioritize the physical and emotional well-being of students and staff. Reflect on strategies to create a safe and nurturing school climate that promotes positive behavior, addresses bullying or harassment, and supports students' social-emotional needs.

8. How can I manage budgetary and human resources effectively? Evaluate the allocation and management of resources, including budgets, staffing, and facilities. Consider different ways to optimize resources and make informed decisions that align with the school's goals and priorities.

9. How can I foster a culture of continuous improvement? Embrace a growth mindset. Reflect on ways to encourage innovation, gather feedback, and use data to inform decision-making and enhance instructional practices.

10. How can I engage in my own self-reflection and professional growth? Recognize the importance of self-reflection and

ongoing professional growth as a leader. Consider strategies to seek feedback, engage in self-assessment, and continuously improve your leadership skills and practices.

By asking themselves these and other critical questions, new principals can set a strong foundation for effective leadership, strategic decision-making, and positive impact on the school community.

Remember, you are not alone in your journey. There are principals across your district, city, state, and country who are willing to help you be successful and not become another statistic of a principal lasting only a year. We are a collaborative group, eager to pick each other up and to see everyone succeed. Utilize your professional network and keep learning. That is both the wonderful and frustrating thing about education. We are never finished and we never arrive. We are constantly moving forward or backward. We never stand still.

There is good work being done each and every day in schools across the country. If you haven't done so already, join The Principal's Desk Facebook group. The conversations in the feed are robust, honest, and earnest. You will get instant feedback on your idea or question whether you like it or not. I urge you to connect with educators in the group who are like-minded and with others who present different opinions and viewpoints. It is in that give-and-take of agreement and discourse where we learn, grow, and broaden our understanding of the complex job we all have undertaken.

Keep these five pillars close in mind. There will be a lot thrown at you during your first year on the job. You will get pulled in a thousand different directions and asked to do a million different things. Don't stray from the five pillars. They will keep you centered, focused, and grounded in what is best for kids.

When principals focus on the five pillars, they act as a multiplier. You may have noticed similarities between the pillars and similar strategies used to address different issues. That is on purpose. You don't need 50 different problems to solve in the first few years of your tenure as principal. By focusing on the five pillars, you will address everything needed to steer a school in the right direction, no matter how lost it was when you got there.

You will always remember that first time you sat down behind the principal's desk. You will always remember the sense of pride, eagerness, and excitement that you will feel in that moment. Let that feeling last as long as possible because before you know it, anxiety, doubt, and stress will come for you. Don't let them in.

You got this.

How do I know?

Because I was once there, too.

References

Arundel, K. (2022). "Home Visits Give Educators and Families Time to Connect." Ed Dive, February 24. https://www.k12dive.com/news/home-visits-give-educators-and-families-time-to-connect/619253/

Battistich, V., Schaps, E. & Wilson, N. (2004). "Effects of an Elementary School Intervention on Students' 'Connectedness' to School and Social Adjustment During Middle School." *The Journal of Primary Prevention 24*(3): 243–262.

Bauer, D. (2022). "Disastrous Leadership: 7 Signs of a Bad Principal." Better Leaders, Better Schools, September 18. https://www.betterleaders betterschools.com/disastrous-leadership-7-signs-of-a-bad-principal/

Birch, S. H. & Ladd, G. W. (1997). "The Teacher–Child Relationship and Children's Early School Adjustment." *Journal of School Psychology 35*(1): 61–79. https://doi.org/10.1016/S0022 4405(96)00029 5

Chen, C.-H., & Yang, Y.-C. (2019). "Revisiting the Effects of Project-based Learning on Students' Academic Achievement: A Meta-analysis Investigating Moderators." *Educational Research Review 26*: 71–81. https://doi.org/10.1016/j.edurev.2018.11.001

Child Mind Institute, Inc. (2015). *Children's Mental Health Report.* https://childmind.org/wp-content/uploads/ChildrensMental HealthReport_052015.pdf

City, E. A., Elmore, R. F., Fiarman, S. E., & Teitel, L. (2009). *Instructional Rounds in Education: A Network Approach to Improving Learning and Teaching*. Cambridge, MA: Harvard Education Press.

Cox, J. W. & Rich, S. (2018). "Armored School Doors, Bulletproof Whiteboards, and Secret Snipers." *Washington Post* (November 13). https://www.washingtonpost.com/graphics/2018/local/school-shootings-and-campus-safety-industry/

Deal, T. E. & Peterson, K. D. (2009). *Shaping School Culture: Pitfalls, Paradoxes, and Promises*. San Francisco: Jossey-Bass.

Curby, T. W., Rimm-Kaufman, S. E. & Ponitz, C. C. (2009). "Teacher–Child Interactions and Children's Achievement Trajectories Across Kindergarten and First Grade." *Journal of Educational Psychology 101*(4): 912–925. https://doi.org/10.1037/a0016647

De Neve, Debbie, Devos, Geert, & Tuytens, Melissa. (2015). "The Importance of Job Resources and Self-efficacy for Beginning Teachers' Professional Learning in Differentiated Instruction." *Teaching and Teacher Education 47*. Doi: 10.1016/j.tate.2014.12.003

Doğan, Selçuk, Pringle, Rose, & Mesa, Jennifer. (2016). "The Impacts of Professional Learning Communities on Science Teachers' Knowledge, Practice and Student Learning: A Review." *Professional Development in Education 42*. Doi: 10.1080/19415257.2015.1065899

Ewing, A. R. & Taylor, A. R. (2009). "The Role of Child Gender and Ethnicity in Teacher–child Relationship Quality and Children's Behavioral Adjustment in Preschool." *Early Childhood Research Quarterly 24*(1): 92–105.

Firestone, W. A. & Wilson, B. L. (1984). *"Creating Cultures That Support Instruction: A View of the Principal's Leadership Role."* Research for Better Schools. Philadelphia, PA.

Godin, S. (2021). As quoted by Danny Bauer in "An Uncommon Approach to Motivating Others: Take Care of Yourself." LinkedIn post (February 17). https://www.linkedin.com/pulse/uncommon-approach-motivating-others-take-care-daniel-bauer-he-him-/

Grissom, J. A., Egalite, A. J., & Lindsay, C. A. (2021). "How Principals Affect Students and Schools." The Wallace Foundation. https://www.wallacefoundation.org/knowledge-center/Documents/How-Principals-Affect-Students-and-Schools.pdf

Hamre, B. K. & Pianta, R. C. (2001). "Early Teacher–child Relationships and the Trajectory of Children's School Outcomes Through Eighth Grade." *Child Development 72*(2): 625–638. https://doi.org/10.1111/1467-8624.00301

Hess, A. J. (2021). "'I Felt Like I Was Being Experimented On': 1 in 4 Teachers Are Considering Quitting After This Past Year," CNBC (June

24). https://www.cnbc.com/2021/06/24/1-in-4-teachers-are-considering-quitting-after-this-past-year.html

Lomos, Catalina, Hofman, Roelande, & Bosker, Roel. (2011). "Professional Communities and Student Achievement – a Meta-analysis." *School Effectiveness and School Improvement 22*: 121–148. Doi: 10.1080/09243453. 2010.550467

Media Smarts. (n.d.). "How Kids Cyberbully." Media Smarts website. https://mediasmarts.ca/digital-media-literacy/digital-issues/cyberbulling/how-kids-cyberbully

Minnich, C. (2022). "Opinion: Data Matters, but Only If It Leads to Effective Teaching Action." Hechinger Report (April 6). https://hechingerreport.org/opinion-data-matters-but-only-if-it-leads-to-effective-teaching-action/

National Crime Prevention Council. (n.d.) *"Stop Cyberbullying Before It Starts."* NCPC website. http://archive.ncpc.org/resources/files/pdf/bullying/cyberbullying.pdf

Newmann & Associates. (1996). *Authentic Achievement: Restructuring Schools for Intellectual Quality.* San Francisco: Jossey-Bass.

Ronfeldt, M., Farmer, S. O., McQueen, K., & Grissom, J. A. (2015). "Teacher Collaboration in Instructional Teams and Student Achievement." *American Educational Research Journal 52*(3): 475–514. https://doi.org/10.3102/0002831215585562

Rudasill, K. M. Reio Jr., T. G., Stipanovic, N. & Taylor, J. E. (2010). "A Longitudinal Study of Student-teacher Relationship Quality, Difficult Temperament, and Risky Behavior from Childhood to Early Adolescence." *Journal of School Psychology 48*(5): 389–412. doi: 10.1016/j.jsp.2010.05.001

Ruder, R. (2006). "Approachability and Visibility." *Principal Leadership 7*(3): 39–41.

Tuckman, B. W. (1965). "Developmental Sequence in Small Groups." *Psychological Bulletin 63*(6): 384–399.

US Department of Education. (2020). "Chronic Absenteeism in the Nation's Schools." https://www2.ed.gov/datastory/chronicabsenteeism.html

Vanblaere, B. & Devos, G. (2018). "The Role of Departmental Leadership for Professional Learning Communities." *Educational Administration Quarterly 54*(1): 85–114. https://doi.org/10.1177/0013161X17718023

Wade, L. (2019). "How Social Media Is Reshaping Today's Education System." *Center for Social Impact Communication.* https://csic.georgetown.edu/magazine/social-media-reshaping-todays-education-system/

Wahlstrom, K., & Louis, K. S. (2008). "How Teachers Perceive Principal Leadership." *Educational Administration Quarterly 44*(4): 498–445.

Walker, T. (2018). "Are Schools Ready to Tackle the Mental Health Crisis?" *NEA News* (September 13). https://www.nea.org/nea-today/all-news-articles/are-schools-ready-tackle-mental-health-crisis

Warwas, J. & Helm, C. (2008). "Professional Learning Communities Among Vocational School Teachers: Profiles and Relations with Instructional Quality." *Teaching and Teacher Education 73*: 43–55. https://doi.org/10.1016/j.tate.2018.03.012

Young, J. (2020). "Researcher Behind '10,000-Hour Rule' Says Good Teaching Matters, Not Just Practice." Edsurge (May 5). https://www.edsurge.com/news/2020-05-05-researcher-behind-10-000-hour-rule-says-good-teaching-matters-not-just-practice

Acknowledgments

The ideas from this book were not created in a vacuum. They were conceptualized over 20 years with many different people contributing to the creation of the five pillars of school leadership.

To all the wonderful educators at Meadowbrook Middle School in Poway, California, and Aviara Oaks Middle School in Carlsbad, California, for guiding me as a new teacher. To the amazing educators at Joseph George Middle School in San Jose, California, and Sequoia Elementary School, in Pleasant Hill, California, thank you for all that you have done for children over the past 20 years and for the support you showed me then as a principal and continue to show me now.

To my graduate professors, Dr. Ray Garcia and Dr. Jose Lopez Lopez, for lighting a fire in me and igniting a passion for school reform and visionary leadership.

To my friends and extended family who have listened to me talk about the contents of this book ad nauseam and read all my posts on social media over the last year: thank you for enduring me.

To my sidekicks, Maggie and Murphy, thank you for keeping me company during long writing sessions and for not barking too much.

To my Dad, for insisting on buying a copy of my last book and this book in person at a physical bookstore.

About the Author

Dr. David Franklin is an award-winning school administrator, education professor, curriculum designer, and presenter. He earned a doctorate in Educational Leadership from California State University, East Bay; a master's in Education Technology from National University; and holds a BA in Music from the University of California, San Diego.

Dr. Franklin is the founder of "The Principal's Desk," an online community of over 230,000 educators from 190 countries.

Dr. Franklin is an education consultant and an adjunct professor of education for Colorado State University, Global Campus. He is also a Marzano Resources associate trained in high reliability schools, instructional rounds, collaborative teams, and PLCs. He has worked with schools and school leaders across the United States as well as internationally on five continents.

Dr. Franklin has presented at national and international education conferences and is a sought-after presenter in the areas of academic intervention, school leadership, creating a shared vision, creating common assessments, and data analysis.

Index

Page numbers followed by *f* indicate figures.

A
active learning:
  defined, 64–65
  minutes per hour, 39, 43,
    88–92, 141
active shooter/intruder
  drills, 183–185
administrative staff, *see* staff
Americans with Disabilities Act
  (ADA), 178
assessment data:
  attendance data, 37–38
  author's experiences
    with, 41–43
  collection/analysis process
    for PLCs, 39–40

  from CWTs, 70–71
  discipline data, 38
  and ELL reclassification, 39
  instructional minutes,
    38–39
  and looking at the right
    data, 37–45
  and Special Education, 39
  student time engaged in
    active learning, 39, 43,
    88–92, 141
assessment for learning, 81–85
  key features of, 83*f*
  types of questions for, 83–84
assessment of
    instruction, 81–85

at-risk students, 171–172,
176, 186–187
attendance, 132–160
author's experiences
with, 157–160
basics of, xix
and creating attendance
plans that work, 145–150
excuses for poor, 134
as factor in academic
performance, 42
and getting butts in
seats, 137–140
holding parents accountable
for, 151–155
and home visits, 141–144
monitoring/evaluation of, 146
real-world methods for
improving, 42–45
and truancy, 133–136, 153–155
attendance data, 37–38
attendance plans:
components of, 146
creating, 145–150
reasons for failure of, 145

B
bathrooms, 148–149
Bauer, Daniel, on leadership's
effect on culture, 22
Bennis, Warren, on leadership, 7
brand identity of school,
104, 106, 192
bullying, 105–106, 187–189
"butts in seats," 38,
42–43, 137–140

C
cafeteria, student-principal
interactions in, 26
calling parents, in order to
praise students,
119–122
cemetery seating, 41, 87–88
chief culture officer
(CCO), 14, 32
child endangerment (legal
definition), 154
choice activities, 63–64
chronic absenteeism, 134–135
classroom layout, 60–61
classrooms, 65–66
classroom walkthroughs
(CWTs), 67–71
climate, culture vs., 164
clothing, 27–28
"coffee with the principal,"
26, 29, 114
colds, effect of, on
attendance, 150
collaboration:
instruction in, 56
between new and
experienced teachers, 17
collaborative culture:
creating, 195–199
vision statement for, 195–197
collaborative leadership:
ideas for developing, 22
top-down vs., 19–22
collaborative learning:
choice activities, 63–64
project-based learning, 63

collaborative partnerships, to support families of immigrant students, 175

collaborative teams, 180–182

collaborative workspaces, 61

collective vision statement, 195–197

colleges and universities, 115

command and control leadership, *see* top-down leadership

communication:
  with families of ELLs, 175
  importance of, in changing school culture, 166–167

communication skills, 56

community, 95–130
  author's experiences with, 127–130
  basics of, xviii–xix
  calling parents with positive news, 119–122
  connecting with, 113–117
  finding, in a new school system, 95–96
  involving businesses/colleges/nonprofits with school, 114–115
  and knowing your neighborhood, 109–112
  and parent–school relationship, 97–99
  school–community research, 97–99
  social media for connecting with, 113–114

social media use in schools, 101–107

support for schools from, 97–99

and video conferencing, 123–125

community liaisons, 42, 127

complicity, legal charge of, 154

compulsory education laws, 153

concrete examples, for teacher development, 16–18

content instruction, ELD and, 173

counterpoint, collaborative leadership and, 22

COVID-19 pandemic, video conferencing and, 123, 124

critical thinking, 56

cultural understanding, ELD and, 173

culture, *see* school culture

CWTs (classroom walkthroughs), 67–71

cyberbullying, 105–106, 187–188

D

Darth Vader leadership style, 19–20

data, *see* assessment data

disciplinary issues, 38, 42, 43, 164. *See also* cyberbullying

discipline data, 38

diversity, and
inclusion, 178–182
dress codes, 27–28
dropping out, truancy
and, 135
Drucker, Peter, on
culture, 163, 198

E
edtech, 73–79
educational neglect, legal
definition of, 153–154
elevator pitch, 196
email, for communicating with
parents, 26
engagement, see student
engagement
English/Language Arts (ELA)
test, 143, 144
English Language Development
(ELD), 39, 171–172
English Language
Learners (ELLs):
and calling parents with
positive news, 122
and inclusion, 171–175
reclassification of, 39
ethics, leadership and, 20
expectations, setting, 55

F
facilitator (PLC team
member), 34
facilities check, 189
families. See also home
visits; parents

and inclusion, 171, 174,
175, 179–180
and school attendance,
134–136, 139, 146
and video
conferencing, 123–125
feedback, positive, calling
parents with, 119–122
first responders, 184
five pillars of school leadership,
xvi–xxi, xviif. See also
attendance; community;
instruction; leadership;
school culture
questions to guide decision-
making, 208–211
flu, effect of, on attendance,
150
food, as means of bringing
people together, 128–129
fun, and school
culture, 201–204

G
Gayle, Crystal, 147
geography, and dress code, 28
Ghosn, Carlos, on
leadership, 7
Gladiator (movie), 165
Gladwell, Malcolm, on 10,000
hour rule, 56–57
Godin, Seth:
on culture, 22
on trust, 163, 197
good news, calling parents
with, 119–122

group norms, PLCs and, 32
group projects, collaborative
   learning and, 62–63

H
Halloween, 202–204
hand sanitizer, 149
health care access, and truancy,
   135–136
hierarchical leadership, *see*
   top-down leadership
home visits:
   conducting, 141–144
   effect of, on academic
      performance, 143–144
   to parents with truant
      children, 42
   as part of
      attendance plan, 148
Hopper, Grace, on culture, 163
hot lunches, helping students
   select, 26
hygiene, 148–149

I
IEP (Individualized Education
   Program) meetings, *see*
   Individualized
   Education Program
   (IEP) meetings
illness, attendance and, 150
immigrants, principals' role in
   supporting, 174. *See also*
   English Language
   Learners (ELLs)
inclusion, 171–182

   of ELL students, 172–175
   of minority students, 178–182
   and responsibilities of
      teachers/staff members,
      180–182
   of students with special
      needs, 175–178
Individualized Education
   Program (IEP) meetings:
   importance of putting
      parents at ease
      during, 176–177
   Special Education and, 39
   video conferencing for
      meetings, 124
instruction, 49–92
   and assessment for
      learning, 81–85
   author's experiences
      with, 87–92
   basics of, xviii
   and classroom observations,
      67–71 (*See also*
      classroom walkthroughs
      (CWTs);
      instructional rounds)
   and effective use of time,
      53–57
   implementing technology
      for, 73–79
   importance of, 49–51
   moving from teacher-led to
      teacher-facilitated, 59–66
   setting expectations for, 55
   and transition from teacher
      to principal, 49–51

instructional minutes:
  as assessment metric,
    38–39, 54
  as factor in truancy, 43
instructional rounds (IRs),
    15, 68–69
intermediaries, collaborative
    leadership and, 22
Internet, and teacher-facilitated
    instruction, 60. *See also*
    social media
interpreters, 122, 144
intruder drills, 183–185
IRs (instructional
    rounds), 15, 68–69

K
Kennedy, John F., on
    leadership, 8
King, Martin Luther, Jr., on
    leadership, 8
Kravitz, Lenny, 25

L
language acquisition/
    development, ELD
    and, 173
law enforcement officers,
    safety protocols
    and, 184
leadership, 3–45
  author's experiences
    with, 41–45
  basics of, xvii–xviii
  becoming a leader, 3–6
  and culture, 13–18

and looking at the right
    data, 37–45
  PLCs and, 31–35
  quotes from well-known
    leaders about, 3–4
  and setting the tone, 13–18
  top-down vs. collaborative,
    19–22, 198–199
  and visibility, 23–29
leadership domain, xx*f*
learning outcomes, redefining
    for technology use,
    74–75
leveled groups, assessment
    results and, 82, 84
libraries:
  public, 115
  school, 180
local businesses, shopping at,
    110–111, 115–116

M
Maxwell, John C., on
    leadership, 8
mental health:
  community-based
    programs, 98–99
  cyberbullying's effect on,
    105–106
  and school safety,
    186–187
mentoring:
  for new principals, 20
  for new teachers, 15–16
mindful mentoring, 15–16
moving, truancy and, 143

music, connecting with
    students via, 25
music programs, xii–xiii

N
Nader, Ralph, on leadership, 7
neighborhood, knowing
    your, 109–112
networking, by new
    principals, 20–21
no-bullying zone, school as, 189
norms, PLCs and, 32
nurses, school, 147–148

O
Obi-Wan Kenobi leadership
    style, 19, 20
outdoor spaces, 61

P
painting classrooms, 198
parenting classes, 152
parents:
    and attendance of elementary
        students, 149
    holding accountable, for
        attendance, 151–155
    and home visits, 141–144
    and information on principal's
        classroom visits, 70
    interaction of, with
        principal, 26–27
    and school–community
        relationship, 97–99
    and video conferencing for
        parent-teacher
        conferences, 123–125

parking lots, 23–24
passive learning, 64. See also
    teacher-led instruction
pay, of teachers and
    administrators,
    167–168
PBL (project-based
    learning), 63–64
Perfect Attendance Award,
    overemphasis on, 150
phone calls:
    to deliver positive
        news, 119–122
    to parents of students of
        tardy/absent
        students, 158–160
pillars of school leadership,
    xvi–xxi, xviif, 208–211.
    See also attendance;
    community; instruction;
    leadership;
    school culture
PLCs, see professional learning
    communities
positive news, calling parents
    with, 119–122
poverty, truancy and,
    135–136, 142
principals:
    average tenure of, 9
    building relationship with
        community, 111
    and creating a collaborative
        culture, 197–199
    and creating collaborative
        learning
        environment, 62

principals: (*continued*)
  and English language
    learners, 173–175
  getting started when hired, 6
  importance of
    leadership role, 7
  reasons for leaving
    position, 9
  and supporting newly
    immigrated
    students, 174
  and supporting students with
    special needs, 177
  turnover rates for, 8
  use of social media by, for
    school–community
    connection, 101–102
Principal's Desk
  network, xv–xvi
privacy, social media and, 105
professional development:
  for ELL instructional
    strategies, 174
  inclusive practices for
    students with special
    needs, 177–178
  instructional rounds
    and, 68–69
  principals' role in
    supporting, 44–45
  veteran teachers and, 17
professional learning
  communities (PLCs),
    xviii, 31–35
  assessments for learning
    and, 84–85

data analysis
  process, 39–40, 44
  sample process for
    instruction/data
    analysis, 33–34
  team roles, 34–35
project-based learning
  (PBL), 63–64
public libraries, 115
pull-out programs, 171–172
push-in programs, 173, 176

R
race, inclusion and, 178–182
reclassification, ELL, 39
recorder (PLC team
  member), 34
relationship-building:
  and communication skills, 56
  with community, xviii–xix,
    97–100, 111, 116
  and inclusive culture,
    179–180, 208
  with parenting classes, 152
  sports and, 25
reporter (PLC team
  member), 34
reputation management, social
  media for, 104
Robb Elementary School, 186
robocalls, to parents of students
  of tardy/absent
  students, 158–160
Rohn, Jim, on leadership, 8
Roosevelt, Eleanor, on
  leadership, 8

S

safe school environment,
    creating a, 183–189
salaries, of teachers and
    administrators,
    167–168
Sandy Hook Elementary
    School, 185
Santa Fe High School, 186
SARB (student attendance
    review board), 133
Saugus High School, 186
scaffolded instruction,
    ELD and, 173
school culture, 163–205
    and attendance, 146–147
    author's experiences
        with, 201–205
    basics of, xix
    climate vs., 164
    and creating a collaborative
        culture, 195–199
    and creating a safe
        environment, 183–189
    defined, 164–165
    importance of, 163–169
    and inclusion, 171–182
    leadership and fostering of, 44
    and principals' role in setting
        tone, 13–18
    and sharing your own story
        via social
        media, 191–193
    trying to change, 165–166
school events, video
    conferencing and, 124

school nurses, student needs
    spotted by, 147–148
science labs, 129
seating layout, for student-lead
    instruction, 60–61
self-directed learning, 104
shooting incidents, drills to
    prepare for, 183–186
shopping, neighborhood–school
    relationships and,
    110–111, 115–116
sick students, 150
Sinek, Simon, on leadership, 7
SMART boards, 76
smiling, 177
soap, 148–149
social media:
    communicating with parents
        via, 26–27
    connecting with community
        via, 113–114
    creating guidelines for, 106
    examples of good posts, 102
    negative student use
        of, 105–106
    positive student use
        of, 103–104
    posts to be avoided, 102
    privacy concerns with, 105
    publicizing a collaborative
        culture with, 199
    for school–community
        connection, 101–107
    and school culture,
        168, 191–193
    toxic positivity on, 167–168

social workers, for addressing
        causes of chronic
        absenteeism, 151–153
Special Education, 39
special needs students, *see*
        students with
        special needs
sports, student-principal
        interactions and, 25
SRO (Student Resource
        Officer), 42, 43
staff:
    and inclusion, 180–182
    and mentorship, 15–16
    and prioritizing classroom
        visits for principal, 69–70
    and safety protocols, 184–185
    and school culture, xix, 8, 13,
        14, 44–45, 165–166
    and social media, 105–106
    and support for ELLs, 174
    support of, for principal's
        CWT, 69–71
    and vision statements, 197
status offense, truancy as, 153
Stoneman Douglas High
        School, 186
student engagement, 43–44
    and attendance, 141, 144, 147
    instruction and, 87–92
    time spent engaged in active
        learning, 39, 43,
        88–92, 141
student-lead instruction, 60–62

Student Resource Officer
        (SRO), 42, 43
students of color, inclusion
        and, 180–182
student support meetings, 124
students with special needs,
        124, 171, 175–178

T
tangible models, for teacher
        development, 16–18
tardiness, 158–160
teachers:
    concepts explained by, with
        real-world examples, 54
    on home visits accompanying
        principals, 143
    and inclusion, 180–182
    percentage of, considering
        quitting, 169
    role of, in creating a
        collaborative
        culture, 198–199
    in schools with positive
        environments, 164
    students' time spent
        with, 53
    turnover rate for, 9, 169
teacher development:
    tangible models for, 16–18
    and teacher
        instruction, 55–56
    three-pronged
        approach to, 14–18

via instructional rounds, 15
via mindful mentoring, 15–16
teacher-facilitated instruction:
  classroom setups for, 65
  and transition to teacher-led
    instruction, 59–66
teacher-led instruction:
  classroom setups for, 65
  and transition to teacher-
    facilitated instruction,
    59–66
teams, collaborative
    leadership and, 22
team development, 181–182
team norms, PLCs and, 32
technology,
    implementing, 73–79
technology committee, 74
10,000 hour rule, 56–57
test scores, at-risk students
    and, 171–172
time:
  effective use of, 53–57
  PLC time as "sacred," 32
timekeeper, on PLC team, 34
tissue etiquette, 149
tone, setting, 13–18
top-down leadership:
  as anathema to collaborative
    culture, 198–199
  collaborative leadership
    vs., 19–22
  deleterious effects of, 20–22
toxic positivity, 166–169

transformational leadership, 20
translators, 122, 144
truancy, xix. *See also* attendance
  and academic
    performance, 42
  definition of, 134
  effects of, 134–136
  legal consequences
    of, 153–155
  prevalence of, among high-
    and middle-school
    students, xix
trust:
  and culture, 163
  and delivering positive news
    to families, 120
  five pillars of (*see* pillars of
    school leadership)
  and interactions with
    families, 55, 127
  for productive teams, 197
  when creating a collaborative
    culture, 197
Twitter, 24

U
universities, 115

V
values, in leadership, 20
veteran teachers:
  support for, 17–18
  and walkthroughs, 67
video conferencing, 123–125

visibility:
  as element of leadership,
    23–29
  putting ideas into action,
    28–29
  student–principal interaction,
    24–26
vision, principals' communi-
    cation of, 10, 45
vision statements, 195–197

W

wages, of teachers and
    administrators,
    167–168
walkthroughs, *see* classroom
    walkthroughs (CWTs)
work dress codes, 27–28
work-life balance, 17–18